I0411544

TABLE OF CONTENTS

Page

ACRONYMS

ARRC   Allied Rapid Reaction Corps

BiH   Bosnia and Herzegovina

CA   Civil Affairs

CAO   Civil Affairs Operations

CIM   Civil Information Management

CIMIC   Civil Military Cooperation

CJCS   Chairman of the Joint Chiefs of Staff

CMO   Civil Military Operations

CMOC   Civil Military Operations Center

EUFOR   European Forces

FHA   Foreign Humanitarian Assistance

FM   Field Manual

GFAP   General Framework Agreement for Peace

HN   Host Nation

IFOR   Implementation Force

IO   Information Operations

MND   Multi-National Divisions

NAM   Non-Alignment Movement

NATO   North Atlantic Treaty Organization

NGOs   Non-Governmental Organizations

PRC   Populace and Resources Control

PSYOP   Psychological Operations

SF   Special Forces

SFOR	Stabilization Force
UN	United Nations
UNPROFOR	United Nations Protection Forces
US	United States
USSR	Union of Soviet Socialist Republics
WWI	World War I
WWII	World War II

CHAPTER 1

INTRODUCTION

This study answers the question, "How effective was United States Civil Affairs in the Bosnian War?" After significant research and analysis the study concluded that United States (US) Civil Affairs (CA), was effective in the Bosnia War. The study examines CA, the history of the region, and how the US military conducted operations in the Bosnian War.

In a world where new conflicts are constantly happening, and one that looks to the US to solve its problems, the US military must be prepared to deal with these events. Worldwide engagement is an immense undertaking and costly in money, time, and lives. Analysis of the Bosnian War indicates the importance of CA capacity to US military operations. CA was employed effectively in the Bosnian War. Understanding the employment of CA capability in the Bosnian War provides insight into the role of these types of units in the future.

In preparing this study the assumption was made that there was accurate recordkeeping. It was also assumed that sufficient sources were available and accessible to uncover the information needed to support the thesis of this study. Typically, organizations keep good records of events and how they unfolded. However there was a chance that the organizations serving in Bosnia either ignored their responsibilities or due to events that happened in the early days of the Internet, records weren't uploaded digitally and were lost. It was also assumed that reputably sources consulted were mostly free of bias.

There were many limitations on conducting this research. These included access to documents, time available, and national level budget issues that caused the Department of Defense to close government facilities and furlough employees during the research and writing of this paper. These shutdowns happened several times during critical stages of work on this project. The most important factor effecting research was the access to relevant documents. The Combined Arms Research Library, Center for Arm Lessons Learned, and faculty of the Command and General Staff College, were the most important resources for researching this paper. Many hours were devoted to searching through the stacks of books in the Combined Arms Research Library and exploiting the digital information that they have retained for student research. Critical members of Center for Army Lessons Learned helped ensure that the most up-to-date information from their archives were available. Still, several weeks of the time available were not used as effectively as possible do to the unforeseen government furloughs.

The topic of CA in Bosnian is very important to the author as a Civil Affairs Officer in the United States Army. It is important to know more about the history of the CA community. As a CA Officer, the author served as a CA Team Leader to the Joint Special Operations Task Force–Philippines, worked with the Filipino Special Forces and conventional military units, and was attached to Task Force Archipelago that was a US Navy SEAL command. The author's past experience as a CA Officer permits him unique insights to the subject of CA employment in the Bosnian War.

This paper examines the effectiveness of CA in the Bosnian War from 1996 to 2004. In order to properly do this, the author researched the roles and responsibilities of the US Civil Affairs in Bosnia. The paper examines the events that led up to the Bosnian

War and the reactions to those events by the US and Europe. It also accounts for the activity of the United Nations (UN) and the North Atlantic Treaty Organization (NATO).

The second chapter focus on US Civil Affairs capabilities. It defines the terms associated with CA operations. There is some confusion in the terms CA, Civil Affairs Operations (CAO), Civil Military Operations (CMO), Civil-Military Cooperation (CIMIC), and when it is appropriate to use them. These terms are important to understand the different organizations and their approaches to the mission in Bosnia. Additionally, this chapter will give a historical overview of the evolution of US Civil Affairs and its applications prior to the Bosnian War.

The third chapter of this paper discusses the history of Bosnia. To understand the conflict of the Bosnian War, it is important to have a grasp of the history of the region. Bosnia is in a region that through history has been influenced by world powers. These external influences affected the different ethnicities of Bosnia and the surrounding nations. During much of the history these ethnicities lived side-by-side in peace and harmony. But in several instances leaders exploited events to wage war on their neighbors for their own benefit. This chapter sets the stage for the beginning of the international community's involvement in the region at the end of the Cold War.

Chapter 4 describes the US and NATO's involvement in the Bosnian War. This chapter illustrates the "Road to War" for the United States and Europe once they realized that action needed to be taken in Bosnia. The chapter will then outline the end state, goals, and objectives both at the strategic and operational level. Chapter 4 focuses on the transition from Implementation Force (IFOR) to Stabilization Force (SFOR) as well as the overall employment of CA in the Bosnian War. A key point in this paper is how CA personnel conducted operations to meet their endstate because this was first time that NATO and US forces utilized CMO and CIMIC operations. This chapter will illustrate how CA personnel and organizations developed operating guidelines to be successful in this environment. This chapter concludes with the transition from NATO led forces to the European Forces (EUFOR) that still occupy Bosnian today.

The fifth chapter looks at the war and operations conducted from the viewpoint of 2013, and evaluates the measures of effectiveness—goals achieved—goals not achieved. The beginning of chapter five assesses the measures of effectiveness by analyzing the goals that had been used to justify the deployment of forces to Bosnia and if they were achieved. This final chapter will also examine the goals and the successes of CA and their actions. Chapter 5 ends with an analysis of the CA lessons of the Bosnian War. The Bosnian War was the first time that US Civil Affairs and NATO CIMIC forces worked together. Almost every future conflict will require CAO, CMO, CIMIC, or stability operations. This study aims to assist in the lowering of redundancies and increasing the efficiency of CA in future conflicts. Taking the lessons from the past will enable CA to be more successful in future endeavors.

Literature Review

Chapter 2 focuses on the doctrine and history of the CA community. In order to present an overview of the doctrine of CA the following manuals were consulted: Joint Publication 3-57, *Joint Doctrine for Civil Affairs*, January 1993; Field Manual (FM) 41-10, *Civil Affairs Operations* (the doctrinal manual from the time of the Bosnian War), September 2013; FM 3-57, *Civil Affairs Operations* (October 2011, the previous version FM 3-05.40); and FM 3-05.401, *Civil Affairs Tactics, Techniques, and Procedures,*

September 2003. Joint Publication 3-57 is the newest joint publication for CA and replaced a 2003 version. This publication serves as a guideline for planning and conducting civil military operations in the joint (multi-service: Army, Navy, Air Force, and Marine) environment. Each one of the service components develops their doctrine independently. This publication is designed to ensure that when the military operates together (joint) they are able to effectively communicate, plan, and execute operations. FM 41-10, was the doctrine at the time of the operation and was published in 1993. It is the most critical document for this chapter and it outlines all the capabilities and structure of the CA units deployed to Bosnia. This publication's target audience was the staff level, especially for planning considerations on how CA conducts operations, and how they could best be employed on the battlefield. The field manuals FM 3-57, and FM 3-05.401 deal specifically with the training, tasks, and procedures of the CA community. Examining the evolutions of the manuals, it shows how the CA community developed their procedures. FM 3-05.401 isn't considered a joint publication, but is used by both the US Army and the US Marine Corps (MCRP 3-33.1A). The focus of this document is the "how to" of the CA community and its supporting operations.

The main sources that were used to illustrate the history of CA was a dissertation written by Dr. DiMarco, "Restoring Order: The U.S. Army Experience with Occupation Operations, 1865-1952," and a series of essays from the Center for Strategic International Studies, International Security Program. Dr. DiMarco's thesis was the primary source for pre-World War II (WWII) CMO applications such as in the Spanish American War, and the Philippine Occupation. The Center for Strategic International Studies is a non-profit organization that provides strategic insight to America's conflicts with a focus on security, transnational, and stability issues. The Center for Strategic International Studies has published *Civil Affairs in WWII*, *Civil Affairs in the Korean War*, *Civil Affairs in the Vietnam War*, *Civil Affairs in Desert Storm*, *Civil Affairs in the Bosnian War*, *Civil Affairs in Haiti*, and the *Future of Civil Affairs*. Each one of the documents portrayed the key issues of the employment of CA and showed the development of CA over time.

Chapter 3 gives the history of Bosnia and Herzegovina. The sources used in this chapter that provided perspective on the Bosnian history were: Noel Malcolm's *Bosnia a Short History*, Robert Donia and John Fine's *Bosnian Hercegovina: A tradition betrayed*, and Carole Roge's *The Breakup of Yugoslavia and the War in Bosnia*. Each one of these books focused on different areas throughout the history of Bosnia that were important to this paper. In Malcolm's *Bosnia a Short History*, most of the useful information was in regards to the Bosnian early history. Malcolm discussed the migration of Slavic settlers into the region. Then he discussed the interaction of these people with each other and the Romans, Byzantines, and Ottomans. He provided the reader with an understanding of the creation of the state and the people of Bosnia. From the beginning he continues to show neighbors and regional powers trying to exert their influence and control over the people of Bosnia.

Robert Donia and John Fine's *Bosnian Hercegovina: A Tradition Betrayed*, carries the story of Bosnia from Ottoman occupation and administration all the way to the end of Tito's reign in 1980. Donia and Fine examine the decay and collapse of the Ottoman's control over Bosnia to the Austro-Hungarian Empire's annexation of Bosnia. One important undercurrent that is repeatedly shown in history is the Serbs attempts to instigate rebellion among the Bosnian people to overthrow their imperial masters. When

6

this is finally accomplished at the end of World War I (WWI), the kingdom of Serbia maneuvers itself to be awarded the rest of the Balkans region from the super powers of the time. This Serbian leadership continues until Tito rises to prominence in WWII and he continues to be the unifying factor until his death in 1980.

Carole Rogel's *The Breakup of Yugoslavia and the War in Bosnia*, picks up with the death of Tito, the power vacuum that it caused, and the tremendous level of violence that was imposed on a once peaceful nation. Like in most cultist situations or dictatorships, there was no groomed successor. Rogel examines the factors that led to the deconstruction of the former state of Yugoslavia.

Chapter 4 focuses on the Bosnian War. The two primary sources used during this chapter were the *Lessons From Bosnia: The IFOR Experience* by Larry Wentz and *Peacekeepers in Bosnia* by Dr. Baumann, George Gawrych, and Walter Kretchik. In *Lessons From Bosnia*, Wentz, who works for the National Defense University, and a team of writers analyzed the IFOR that was deployed in support of the Dayton Accords. They provide a detailed depiction of IFOR's operations between the years of 1995 and 1997. The team then took a more in-depth analysis of IFOR by functions. The chapters that were the most useful were "Civil-Military Cooperation" and "Lesson's Learned about Lessons Learned." The second book that was used for chapter 4 was *Peacekeepers in Bosnia,* which is a Combat Studies Institute book written by Dr. Bauman, George Gawrych, and Walter Kretchik. This was by far one of the most important sources to the research. The book looks at the history of the Balkans region, Yugoslavia (royal and communist), and the modern state of Bosnia and Herzegovina. The book then covers United Nations Protection Forces (UNPROFOR), IFOR, and SFOR; bringing out a tremendous level of detail and analysis. The authors were able to draw their conclusions based off their entrée to the student body at Command and General Staff College at Fort Leavenworth. Many of the topics and the conclusion in the book were backed up by interviews that were conducted with the people intimately involved at all levels of operations. It would be hard for me to say which section or chapter I focused on because each part of the book played an important role in the writing of this paper.

Chapter 5, the final chapter, focuses on the measures of effectiveness of CA in the Bosnian War. This chapter relies mainly on the sources used in previous chapters.

CHAPTER 2

CIVIL AFFAIRS

Civil Affairs is a complex organization with a dynamic mission set. Several times in the US ' military history, after victory, the leadership had to ask themselves' "now what?" Inevitably leaders turned to the CA units to begin reconstruction, stabilization, or develop the host nation (HN) to be able to be self-reliant. This chapter provides an overview of CA, a doctrinal look at CAO, and the history of CA.

Overview of Civil Affairs

The term Civil Affairs refers to a type of unit and a branch within the Army. CA units execute Civil Affairs Operations, which are specific task sets that CA units are exclusively trained to conduct. Civil Military Operations is a line of effort that a commander plans to execute in support of his unit's mission. All units can conduct CMO, where as CAO is exclusive to CA units.[1]

Throughout the history of the US military, CA units have fulfilled many different critical mission sets. The activities that CA has been responsible for include heading critical civil agencies; coaching foreign agencies or teaching them how to reconstruct their own systems; taking care of people during an emergency; and developing the civilian layer of the operational picture.[2] The success of CA units has created a strong

---

[1]U.S. Department of the Army, Field Manual (FM) 3-57 (replaced Field Manual 3-05.40), *Civil Affairs Operations* (Washington, DC: Government Printing Office, 2011), 1-1–1-6.

[2]U.S. Department of the Army, Field Manual (FM) 3-05.40, *Civil Affairs Operations* (Washington, DC: Government Printing Office, October 2006), 1-2–1-6.

reputation of "can do" capability that has been applied over the entire world in many conflicts. To understand how CA has been so successful it is important to understand the doctrine of CA, which has not changed significantly since the Bosnian War.

Civil Affairs Operations

Civil Affairs Operations develop the environment in which the military operates. The operational environment extends beyond military units or assets and includes the civilian populace. By using CAO, CA units can influence the populace to support the commander's mission. With proper application of CAO, CA units can turn the civilian population into a force multiplier. CAO has been used as a part of many counter-insurgency strategies. Within CAO there is five core tasks: Populace and Resources Control (PRC), Foreign Humanitarian Assistance (FHA), Civil Information Management (CIM), Nation Assistance, and Support to Civil Administration. These are all critical to CA's mission accomplishment.

Populace and Resources Control is the act of controlling the populace and the resources needed to support that population. PRC is critical during a state of emergency or conflict. There are several types of missions that CA units conduct in support of PRC: "Identifying or evaluating existing host nation PRC measures. Advising on PRC measures that would effectively support the commander's objectives. Recommending command guidance on how to implement PRC measures. Identify and assess Measures of Effectiveness (MOEs) and Measure of Performance (MOPs). Participating in the execution of selected PRC operations, as needed or directed. Assisting in the arbitration of problems arising from implementation of PRC measures."[3] PRC can be one of the

most difficult tasks, because it can require cooperation with many separate entities with

competing agendas.

Foreign Humanitarian Assistance is the act of conducting humanitarian assistance

in a foreign country as a result of a natural or manmade disaster. Typically, this type of

operation is conducted in support of the HNs and the international community's effort to

support the effected population. FHA missions can include providing security (allowing

civilian agencies to operate safely and uninhibited), conducting assessments, and

"providing specific military capabilities applied in direct disaster relief roles (providing

food and medical care, constructing basic sanitation facilities, repairing public facilities,

constructing shelters and temporary camps, and helicopter and fixed-wing transport for

supplies, commodities, and passengers as demonstrated by the Indian Ocean Tsunami

response in 2004–2005)."[4] Most CA missions that are conducted abroad have some type

of FHA package embedded in them. These can range from a small ad hoc gesture from

the civil affairs team to a multinational interagency medical civil action program that

requires a flotilla to support it.

Civil Information Management is the collection and analysis of information in

regard to the civilian aspect of the operational environment. The collection can be done

on the civilian population from media sources, various assessments, key leader

engagements, or conducting civil reconnaissance. One of CA most critical tasks is being

---

[3]U.S. Department of the Army, Field Manual (FM) 3-57, 3-2.

[4]Ibid., 3-6.

able to bring all this information together and determining what the commander needs to know in order to be successful at his mission.[5]

Nation Assistance operations are designed to support a HN's effort to increase stability within their borders. The subordinate programs within Nation Assistance are security assistance, foreign internal defense, and programs conducted by other federal agencies. Security assistance deals with training and equipping foreign militaries to enhance their capabilities. Foreign internal defense operations are in support of the HN's ability protect itself from insurgency or lawlessness within their borders.[6]

Support to Civil Administration operations are utilized to support or stabilize a government or agencies of the HN. Support to Civil Administration operations can be divided into two types of missions, those conducted in a friendly territory or those conducted in an occupied territory. In a friendly territory CA forces will assess, give assistance, mentor, and coach the HN agencies in their efforts.[7] In the occupied territories the CA forces will augment the HN or occupation government, this was done extensively in WWII.[8]

During the Bosnian War, CA employed FHA, CIM, and Support to Civil Administration. FHA was one of the few aspects of CAO that was being applied before deployment of forces on the ground by Operation Provide Comfort. Even though the

---

[5]Ibid., 3-10.

[6]Ibid., 3-13.

[7]Ibid., 3-17–3-18.

[8]U.S. Department of the Army, Field Manual (FM) 41-10, *Civil Affairs Operations* (outdated version) (Washington, DC: Government Printing Office, 1993), 1-11.

scope of its operations were limited US forces provided air lift assets to deliver humanitarian aide to Sarajevo, that was distributed by Non-Governmental Organizations (NGOs) that were operating in the area. Once on the ground and deployed throughout the battlefield CA executed FHA in coordination with relief agencies to distribute aide to populations in need. CA employed CIM during the Bosnian War by passing the information they acquired during their missions to the respective intelligence gathering departments. CIM was initially done passively, but as the US forces' commitments deepened, CIM was used to gain measurements of effectiveness during operations. CA also executed many of its specialties of Support to Civil Administration in Bosnian. CA's capabilities to bring civilian expertise to the battlefield were initially marginalized due to the fear of mission creep. Once the transition of priorities led to stabilization CA was allowed to employ Support to Civil Administration to all aspects of the Bosnian operating environment.

Civil Affairs Structure

As US Civil Affairs units were alerted for duty in Bosnia, the force structure was much different than it is today (2013). The CA branch was both an Active Duty and a Reserve Component. CA units were organized into teams, companies, battalions, and brigades. Since Bosnia, CA unit structure has evolved and will likely continue to undergo changes in the near future.

During the Bosnian War, the CA structure was significantly heavier in the Reserve Component. The Active Duty component only had a one battalion the 96th Civil Affairs Battalion (Airborne) (96th CA BN (A)) stationed at Fort Bragg, and functional area staff officers in some operational headquarters around the world.[9] Each one of the 96th CA BN (A)'s companies was regionally aligned and their soldiers were trained in language and various cultural aspects of those regions. The functional area staff officers, were for the most part, only on temporary duty to be released back to their parent branch after certain period of time.

The reserve CA had five Civil Affairs Brigades: 351st, 352nd, 353rd, 358th, and 361st.[10] Even though these reserve CA Brigades maintained a certain amount of regional orientation, their real value came in the form of their expertise in 20 civilian fields.[11] These fields typically mirrored the individual CA soldier's civilian occupation. This ensured that the soldiers were aware of the most current and effective application of their skill set. For example, soldiers in the reserve civil affairs "legal" skill set held civilian jobs as paralegals, lawyers, and even judges.[12] This allowed them to be able to apply their expertise to reconstruct or develop foreign nations capabilities with little or no additional training once brought to Active Duty.

History of Civil Affairs

Is the state made up of people or do the people make the state? Either way the state imposes its will upon the civilian populous frequently by means of its military. Since the beginning of warfare civilians have influenced the battle plans of commanders.

---

[9]Ibid., 4-1.

[10]Ibid., 5-5.

[11]Ibid., 4-12–4-16.

[12]Ibid., 4-14.

Some of these commanders protected their cities, towns, or villages. This ensured that the peasants could pay taxes to fund the state, or the military needed to sack an opposing city in order to gain wealth for their own state. Over time militaries have figured out ways to influence the population, unfortunately for the majority of history militaries used fear or terror tactics to influence the civil population. Several examples of military leaders exist in history who have made the connection between an amicable civilian population, stability, and the increase in power for their own state. One of these military leaders was Alexander the Great, who was respected for his ability to understand how to treat conquered people. Once he conquered a group of people he assimilated them and made them part of his empire. This gave the people the feeling that they had a share in the empire.[13] These benign military conquests set an early example of the positive effects of well conceived civil affairs operations.

Theoretically the development of civil affairs in the United States of America started with the first settlers. They had the ability to influence the local people, who allowed them to settle on the their land. Achieving the early settlements without general warfare was a great accomplishment. This is especially true since some of the native American tribes were based on a warrior culture. After the foundation of the US, the American military used civil affairs in various forms from the Revolutionary War until the late 1800s. The primary focus of CAO was on pacifying indigenous people in order to expand the union from coast to coast. Often pacification attempts failed due to deceiving or mistreatment of the local inhabitants by the US Government or because the objectives of the US Government and Native American were not reconcilable. Military force was

---

[13]Ibid., 1-10.

15

thus an aspect of the interaction between the government and the Native Americans. By 1890, the US had pacified or marginalized America's indigenous tribes.[14]

As America extended its influence outside its continental boarders, it developed ways for the military to interact with foreign governments and foreign populations. One of the earliest examples of the US military developing civil military policy, in regard to foreign civilians, can be attributed General Winfield Scott in 1847. During the war with Mexico "his vision of the basic conduct of operations and establishment of stable relations with the Mexican populace under General order No. 20, which required his troops to respect the rights and property of Mexicans, local government, and the Roman Catholic Church,"[15] ensued harmonious relations between the US Army and the Mexican civilian populations. This view of respecting the local civilian population reduced their interference in military operations and allowed the military increased freedom to operate in these areas.

The next major foreign conflict in American history was the Spanish American War of 1898. After the US defeated the Spanish military, the US needed to figure out what do to with Cuba, Guam, and the Philippines. In the case of Cuba, America wanted to hand the country back over to its inhabitants and to allow American businesses to benefit from Cuban markets and resources. The President of the US appointed General Leonard Wood as Military Governor. His main task was to "restore order, prepare the

---

[14]Louis DiMarco, "Restoring Order: The US Army Experience with Occupation Operations, 1865-1952" (PhD diss., Kansas State University, 2010), 98.

[15]W. Baron, "Civil Affairs United States of America," *CIMIC Messenger*, no. 1 (March 2013), http://www.cimic-coe.org/download/newsletter/CIMIC-Messenger-2013-01-final.pdf (accessed July 13, 2013).

country for economic and individual prosperity."[16] Once again this was a great opportunity for a commander to be able to influence the population in a non-kinetic manner.

In order to accomplish the task that he had been given, General Wood developed the foundation of modern day civil affairs. In addition, the progressive movement of equality and the "common man" versus the elite had begun to influence American politics. An example of the rise of progressivism was the presidency of Theodore Roosevelt and his success in his "Trust-busting" campaign. Wood used progressive ideas as the backbone of his policies as the Governor of Cuba. He focused on creating a government of elected native officials and building the critical civil infrastructure needed to support the development of the state. Wood focused on the development of a population centric approach, one in which the population takes over the administration and becomes self-reliant. The system that Wood developed in Cuba was very successful and the locals embraced the idea. However, with limited resources, personnel, and the military's focus turning to the Philippine-American War, the American's withdrew their forces from Cuba in 1902. The withdrawal was premature because shortly after the departure of the US forces, chaos ensued. The premature departure of American military forces was one of the causes of a half-century of Cuban political instability.[17]

The US acquired the Philippine Islands as part of the treaty with Spain after the Spanish-American War. Initially, the Filipino people welcomed the Americans as

---

[16]Colonel Jayne A. Carson, "Nation-Building, The American Way" (Strategy Research Project, United States Army War College, Carlisle Barracks, PA, 2003), http://www.fas.org/man/eprint/carson.pdf (accessed October 19, 2013).

[17]DiMarco, "Restoring Order," 132-135.

liberators. But the US couldn't decide what it wanted to do with the Philippines. The options were to annex it to another regional power, give it independence, or annex the Philippines into the United States. The general feeling was that the Filipinos couldn't govern themselves, the islands were vulnerable to other regional powers, and that the US needed unrestricted access to Asian ports for its Navy and commercial interests. General Dewey was the commander that eliminated Spanish influence over the Philippines. He felt that the best option would be to support the Filipino revolutionaries and allow them to take control of their own country, as long as America had access to its ports and economy. The American officials in Washington were more interested in controlling all aspects of Philippine governance. Because of this policy the US military was forced to impose US governance on the Philippines by force. By 1902 the US military had quelled the "Philippine Insurrection" and established US led governance. This approach marginalized the will of the people of the Philippines.

During the years that America governed the Philippines there were many famous leaders (William Taft and General Arthur MacArthur) that participated in the stabilization of the Philippines. Geographically there were over 7,000 islands in the Filipino archipelago, many different conflicting ethnicities, and they previously had a decentralized government that was rife with corruption and cronyism. During the period of US governance the US military employed CMO to influence the population. CMO included building roads, school, ports, and educational programs. The military gained a great amount of experience in CMO during this campaign that would be applied later in WWII, by leaders such as Douglas MacArthur and George Marshall, both of whom served in the Philippines. The Philippines were effectively administrated by the US, first by a US military government from 1899 to 1901, then transitioned to a US civil governor supported by the US Army, and finally as a commonwealth until its independence in 1946.[18] Due to the military's focus on the people instead of the enemy during this occupation, bonds were created between the two nations, which still has relevance in the Philippines today.

World War I was the beginning of the end to the era of empires. Each one of the European powers was locked into treaties that would require them to defend their allies against aggression. The level of violence in WWI had never been seen before in history. When the fighting was done and the treaties were sign, the US had to occupy a section of Germany. During the occupation of the Rhineland by American forces, the American military needed to conduct CAO and CMO and were woefully unprepared. As Colonel Irwin L. Hunt, Officer in Charge of Civil Affairs, Third Army states, "the American army of occupation lacked both training and organization to guide the destinies of the nearly one million civilians whom the fortunes of war had placed under its temporary sovereignty."[19] This statement was part of the "Hunt Report" and alerted the US leadership that the military needed to prepare itself in advance of any future conflicts that would require occupation or reconstruction efforts. During the years between WWI and WWII, Army doctrine began to incorporate these ideas and produced the Rules of Land Warfare in 1936 and the US Marine Corps published the "Small Wars Manual."[20] This doctrinal work helped prepare the US military for WWII.

---

[18]Ibid., 170-176.

[19]Baron, "Civil Affairs United States of America."

[20]Ibid.

At the beginning of WWII the American leadership began to develop its CAO and CMO capabilities with the establishment of the School of Military Government and the activation of the Civil Affairs Division.[21] This school and the accompanying doctrine shaped the CA into becoming one of the most critical aspects of planning and training for all the allied campaign of WWII. CA personnel were operating at every level of the military, from the high-level staff positions advising commanders to the tactical level implementation of programs. This was the first war in which CA efforts were utilized on a grand scale. Instead of being a supporting or marginal effort, CA moved into the forefront of the stabilization and reconstruction effort. As soon as the Axis forces had been defeated in the area CAO began. In both theaters of WWII Civil Affairs units were tasked to support the civilian population, establish military governments and supporting systems, and keep the civilians from interfering with on going operations.[22]

The US Civil Affairs adopted two main strategies in reconstruction during and after WWII, the direct and indirect approach.[23] The indirect approach was preferred because it required less assets and minimal military involvement in civilian systems. This approach was used in areas that had been liberated such as Belgium, the Netherlands, and Luxembourg. With this approach it allowed for exiled leadership to recover the existing structures and resources of a government in order to self govern. This approach was also

---

[21]Ibid.

[22]Cristen Oehrig, *Civil Affairs in World War II* (Washington, DC: Center for Strategic and International Studies), http://csisdev.forumone.com/files/media/csis/pubs/090130_world_war_ii_study.pdf (accessed July 13, 2013).

[23]Ibid.

used in Japan, as the "top-down" driven methods preferred by General Douglas MacArthur, where CA units were used to assist, assess, and to mentor local officials.[24]

The direct approach was required in Germany where the de-Nazification resulted in the removal of significant portions of the population from being involved in reconstruction efforts, in addition to the collapse of all civil services with the end of Hitler's regime.[25] Due to the uprooting of the existing governance systems, CA was needed to administer the state and local levels of government directly.[26]

An example of civil affairs' success in the Pacific Theater was on Okinawa. Previously, the people of Okinawa were told by the Japanese propaganda that US forces would rape all the women, kill all the men, and "send the children and elderly to the San Francisco to be ground into meat."[27] In addition, the Japanese forces gave the Okinawan people minimal rations, told them to hide in the hills or caves, and when the Americans arrived to attack them or kill themselves. The success of the civil affairs personnel working with the surviving civilian population demonstrated that Allied forces were not there to rape and slaughter the people. The way in which these units and personnel conducted themselves was critical to reducing the amount of insurgents in the occupied areas to virtually zero. In a short time the Allied forces accumulated masses of refugees because of the trust that they had build with the locals that they had encountered. As

---

[24]Ibid.

[25]Ibid.

[26]Ibid.

[27]Special Operations History Foundation, "Objective Security," Recorded 1945, United States Marine Corps, film strip, http://specialoperationshistory.info/omeka/items/ show/124 (accessed May 21, 2013).

combat operations continued to rage on the southern part of the Okinawa, the civil affairs personnel got the local population back to work at reconstructing the other parts of the island. They motivated the locals to do all the work by themselves and with their own supplies. This was because all military material that was being brought to the island was needed for military operations.

The US had a longer-term interest in Okinawa, because the US built military installations to create a strategic footprint in Asia. Investing in the people of Okinawa from the first minute US forces landed on the island to free them from the Imperial Japanese reduced the chance of insurgency, won the confidence of the people, and thus maintained a critical capability in Asia. The US control of Okinawa was not relinquished until 1972. Throughout the history of US control of the island, CAO was critical to harmonious relations between the US and the foreign civilian population.

At the end of WWII, the Allied forces liberated the nation of Korea, which had been occupied by Japan for 40 years. The main difficulty in Korea was that the North and the South had significantly different views of what type of regime should rule the new nation. The victorious nations of WWII decided to split the country along the 38th parallel. The north region was assisted by its northern neighbor, the Soviet Union, and adopted a form of communism. The southern region was initially placed under the Army Military Government (United States of America Military Government in Korea), by the US using the direct governance method.[28] In 1948, South Korea elected its first president, the United States of America Military Government in Korea was dissolved and the US

---

[28]Audrey Villinger, *Civil Affairs in the Korean War* (Washington, DC: Center for Strategic and International Studies), http://csis.org/files/media/csis/pubs/ 090130_korea_study.pdf (accessed July 14, 2013).

began using a more indirect approach to support the Republic of Korea.[29] In 1950 North Korea invaded the Republic of Korea. The Korean conflict involved the UN, China, 16 western allies, and caused the death of hundreds of thousands of people. CA in the Korean War was mainly focusing on the large amount of displaced civilians, economic issues, and public health issues, in support of the Republic of Korea Government. CA structured their efforts in three phases: achieve peace, reestablish normal political and economic conditions (as long as they didn't impede US military objectives), and a reunified government of Korea to hold free elections.[30] In the end both sides signed an armistice and created a demilitarized zone generally along the pre-war border. CA effectiveness in the Korean War continued to illustrate its importance to US strategy in times of war.[31]

As the Cold War continued, America committed forces globally to stop the spread of communism. After the Korean War, the next hot spot was Vietnam where a communist insurgency had been going on for several years. In Vietnam the US had two distinct strategies for two different types of enemy: "A conventional battle strategy against the People's Army of North Vietnam (PAVN) and a counterinsurgency battle in the south against the smaller Viet Cong (VC) insurgency."[32] The strategy against the conventional People's Army of North Vietnam forces was one that the military had trained for. The US

---

[29]Ibid.

[30]Ibid.

[31]Ibid.

[32]Kathleen Hicks and Christine Wormuth, *The Future of U.S. Civil Affairs* (Washington, DC: Center for Strategic and International Studies), http://csis.org/files/publication/130409_Hicks_FutureCivilAffairs_Web.pdf (accessed July 14, 2013).

pursued a strategy of attrition. In the conventional fight, General Westmoreland's strategy was generally successful. The counterinsurgency strategy was one of the first times that the US developed a strategy that was aimed at the civilian population. The strategy was built around the Civil Operations and Revolutionary Development Support program. The Civil Operations and Revolutionary Development Support program had three main objectives: "Eliminate the VC insurgency in South Vietnam; Diminish the VC's ability to recruit; Recruit indigenous tribes to fight the VC and the NLF."[33] Even though the outcome of Vietnam was not favorable to the US, the Civil Operations and Revolutionary Development Support program was successful for the development of CA, in that it developed interagency and intergovernmental efforts to a common goal.[34]

After Vietnam, CA was employed exclusively in support of Special Operations missions. This allowed CA personnel to participate in small conflicts to continue to develop their tactics, technics, and procedures during the stalemate of the Cold War. The conflicts in El Salvador, Grenada, and Panama are examples of CA being used in a limited and indirect role, but being very successful.[35]

In the 1990s America and its allies came to the defense of Kuwait as a result of the Iraqi invasion. Initially CA played a minor role, because the mission was to remove the Iraq forces and reinstate the Kuwait Administration. Once the Allied forces retook Kuwait, the coalition command realized that the HN was in desperate need of help with

---

[33]Ibid.

[34]Dale Andrade and James H. Willbank, "CORDS/Phoenix: Counterinsurgency Lessons from Vietnam for the Future," *Military Review* (March-April 2006): 9-23.

[35]Hicks and Wormuth, *The Future of U.S. Civil Affairs.*

its ability to provide essential services. The main issues were caring for the displaced

civilians and the restoration of the infrastructure, mainly the power grid.[36] Since CA had

created these skills in WWII and had been developing them ever since, they were well

equipped for the mission and contributed to reconstruction and reestablishment of the

Kuwait Government and economy.

In 1993 with the passing of the Cohen-Nunn Act and the creation of US Special

Operations Command, CA became part of the special operations branch.[37] When Haitian

president Jean-Bertrand Aristide was ousted from power, a (US-led) UN task force was

deployed in 1994 to reinstate him. This mission should have been tailor made for CA

forces, unfortunately, there were many problems with planning, coordination, and

communication with all the entities involved. Even with the problems and set backs the

mission was considered a success for civil affairs as they completed all their objectives

and hundreds of projects in support of the HN.[38] The Haiti mission helped US CA focus

on large-scale contingency operations. It was a great opportunity to prepare the CA focus

for large missions. That same year conflict began to flare up in former Yugoslavia, which

will be discussed in depth in the next chapter.

---

[36]Eric Ridge, *Civil Affairs in Desert Shield/Storm* (Washington, DC: Center for Strategic and International Studies), http://csis.org/files/media/csis/pubs/090129_desert_shield_desert_storm_study.pdf (accessed November 5, 2013).

[37]Hicks and Wormuth, *The Future of U.S. Civil Affairs.*

[38]Jeremy Patrick White, *Civil Affairs in Haiti* (Washington, DC: Center for Strategic and International Studies), http://csis.org/files/media/csis/pubs/090130_haiti_study.pdf (accessed November 5, 2013).

CHAPTER 3

GOALS AND OBJECTIVES FOR THE BOSNIAN WAR

<u>The History of Bosnia and the Greater Yugoslavia</u>

To understand Bosnia and the challenges contained in conducting CAO in Bosnia, one needs to understand Yugoslavia, the Slavic people, religious demographics, and the history of the region. For most of its history Bosnia has been dominated by an external regional power, it had been part of the "Roman empire, then Charlemagne, then the Ottomans, the Austro-Hungarians, and finally the Slavs ruled it politically. The faiths of the Western Christians, Eastern Christians, Judaism, and Islam" all influenced it religiously.[39] The earliest historical account of this area is from the Greeks who referred to the people of the region as the "Illyrians."[40] The Illyrian Tribe inhabited the area known as Yugoslavia and Albania. The Illyrians were conquered by the Romans in 9 AD and created the Roman Province of Dalmatia.[41] The Romans brought Christianity and established the first bishops in the first century.[42] Around the third and fourth century AD, the Roman Empire began to decay and eventually Rome was sacked by the

---

[39]Noel Malcolm, *Bosnia A Short History* (New York: New York University Press, 1994), xix.

[40]Ibid., 2.

[41]Ibid.

[42]Ibid.

Visigoths in 410 C.E.[43] This created a power vacuum which allowed many previously repressed ethnic groups to migrate around modern day Europe including Bosnia.

Around this time, the Byzantine Empire rose to prominence. Byzantine Emperor Justinian conquered the geographic area that became Bosnia in attempts to reclaim Rome's lost lands, in the name of Christianity.[44] During this same period there was a regional influx of Turks and Huns. These ethnic migrant groups were not a conquering army, but they had an important impact on the regions ethnic make up. In the sixth century AD, there was a large migration of Slavs that moved from their homeland in central and Eastern Europe into the Balkans. The first waves of immigrants came from Slaveni as settlers.[45] Later, another wave of Slav tribes came into the region. These tribes would become known as the Croats and Serbs, who dominated the earlier Slavic immigrants.[46] This shared Slavic heritage would be a cause of conflict in the future as the rival groups tried to prove their superior ethnic purity.

Around the ninth century AD the Croats were Christianized under the Byzantine Empire.[47] At the same time Charlemagne's Franks invaded and conquered part of northwestern Bosnia, which caused the western European system of feudalism to be

---

[43]Ushistory.org, "The Fall of the Roman Empire," http://www.ushistory.org/civ/ 6f.asp (accessed August 22, 2013).

[44]Malcolm, *Bosnia A Short History*, 4.

[45]Robert Donia and John Fine, *Bosnia Hercegovina: A Tradition Betrayed* (New York: Columbia University Press, 1994), 13-14.

[46]Ibid., 71-72.

[47]Malcolm, *Bosnia A Short History*, 8.

introduced to the region.[48] Serbia was developing into princedoms by the mid-tenth century and began to encroach from the west, under the acknowledgement of Byzantine sovereignty. This was the first time that history recorded the name Bosnia. The Byzantine Emperor Constantine Porphyrogenitus discussed the lands that had been bestowed upon a Serbian Prince, using that name. The Byzantines considered Bosnia to be inherently Serbian, but shortly after in 960 AD it fell under Croatian rule and remained with them for roughly a half century.[49]

Bosnia for many years went back and forth between Croat, Serb, and other foreign power's control.[50] Around 1180 with the demise of the Byzantine Empire as a regional power and the rise of the Hungarian kingdom, Bosnia escaped the control of the Serbs and Croats.[51] This was due to the collapse of the Byzantines that weakened the Serbs while the Hungarians (who controlled Croatia) were consolidating their power. This was the first time that Bosnia achieved the status of an independent state.[52] Still, despite Bosnian independence, the state had significant connections to the Serbs, Croats, and the larger Slav ethnic community. Due to its distance from the power centers of the time, Bosnia was allowed to develop an independent identity during this period.[53]

---

[48]Ibid., 9.

[49]Ibid., 10.

[50]Ibid.

[51]Ibid.

[52]Ibid.

[53]Donia and Fine, *Bosnia Hercegovina*, 17.

Bosnian development during the medieval times (1180 to 1463) had three significant rulers: Ban Kulin, Stephen Kotormanic, and King Stephen Tvrtko.[54] Under the second and third rulers Bosnia expanded to be the most powerful state in the western Balkans.[55] The Ban Kulin period in history was a peaceful one. He managed diplomatic relationships with Serbia and the Hungarians (who were now firmly in control of the Croats). During this time church politics, not war was the main form of conflict. Bosnia's neighbors (Hungry and several other states) petitioned Rome to be authorized to absorb Bosnia into its jurisdiction. This eventually led to Hungary's invasion of Bosnia in the 1230s. In a beneficial twist of events, the Hungarian invasion forces had to retreat shortly after the invasion began to protect Hungry from the invading Mongols. The Mongols destroyed the Hungarian forces and proceeded to plunder the region. However, due to the death of the Great Khan, the Mongol Army returned home, leaving Bosnia largely untouched.[56] For the rest of this period Bosnia remained stable in the region, except for some interference from Hungry in regards to the running of the Catholic dioceses.

Stephen Kotormanic came to power in Bosnia in 1318 and he expanded his power to include Herzegovina in 1326.[57] He managed the relationship with neighboring powers to ensure that they would not be tempted to invade his lands.[58] During his reign Kotormanic was wise enough to realize that the survival of his kingdom relied on

---

[54]Malcolm, *Bosnia A Short History*, 13.

[55]Ibid.

[56]Ibid., 16.

[57]Ibid., 283.

[58]Ibid., 17.

allowing the larger religious powers to conduct their business and not interfere with either the Catholics or the Christian Orthodox.[59] Kotormanic left a prosperous and independent Bosnia behind when he died in 1353.[60]

The last of the three rulers was Stephen Tvtrko. He was plagued by revolts and Hungarian land seizures from the onset of his reign.[61] In time Tvtrko was able to diplomatically influence the Hungarian King into a sort of alliance, allowing him to focus on his southern border with Serbia. Serbia had been encountering difficulties from within, and Tvtrko took advantage of this weakness by offering assistance in return for land and position in the Serbian kingdom. In addition, Tvtyko used the surrounding states weaknesses to his advantage by brokering treaties and creating small alliances, which eventually gave him control of the coastline and some of the islands in the Adriatic Sea.[62]

In 1388, Turkish raiding parties began to penetrate the region and wiped out some of the local armies. Prince Lazar of Serbia turned to the Bosnian King Tvtrko for military assistance. Tvtrko sent an army to assist in the defense of Serbia in the "Battle of Kosovo." The Serbian and Bosnian armies were defeated and Prince Lazar was captured and executed by the Turks.[63] The battle was a draw, but strategically it was a severe defeat for Serbia, because they lacked the ability to reconstitute their forces and within six months the Turkish forces of the Ottoman Empire had returned to conquer Serbia.

---

[59]Donia and Fine, *Bosnia Hercegovina*, 20.

[60]Malcolm, *Bosnia A Short History*, 13.

[61]Donia and Fine, *Bosnia Hercegovina*, 28.

[62]Malcolm, *Bosnia A Short History*, 17.

[63]Ibid., 20.

King Tvtrko and his descendants made treaties and agreements with the Ottomans in order to stay in power under the Ottoman Empire.[64] Christianity in the region was overshadowed by the Ottoman Empire conquering kingdoms and reducing the Churches ability to reach the people. In 1463, the Ottoman Empire conquered Bosnia and killed its king. Soon after the defeat, the main Turkish forces withdrew and the Hungarian kingdom quickly invaded and took control of the area.[65] The area would go back and forth between Hungarian (now under the Hapsburg family) and Ottoman control, with the locals having to pay tribute in gold and people to both empires.

Since the beginning of Islam's expansion, there has always been some interaction with Muslims, but nothing on a grand scale. As the Ottoman Empire took control of the region there was a steady increase in the Muslim population. In addition, the collapse of the Byzantine Empire left a power void in the Christian Orthodox communities. The Ottoman Empire filled this void by presenting their newly conquered people with a state sponsored religion.[66] From 1520 to 1550 there was a push for conversion to Islam and the Muslim population rose to f 40 percent.[67] In the next 150 years the Muslim population continued to displace the Christians (both Catholic and Orthodox) in Bosnia.[68] The

---

[64]Ibid.

[65]Donia and Fine, *Bosnia Hercegovina*, 284.

[66]Maya Shatziller, *Islam and Bosnia: Conflict Resolution and Foreign Policy in Multi-Ethnic States* (Ontario, Canada: McGill-Queen's University Press, 2002), 7.

[67]Malcolm, *Bosnia A Short History*, 17.

[68]Ibid., 54.

Ottoman Empire favored the Orthodox Christians over the Roman Catholics.[69] This favoritism was due to the fact that the Orthodox Church was firmly under the control of the Ottoman Empire and had no state that was sponsoring its people. In contrast, the Catholic Church was deeply allied with the ruling political powers of Western Europe.

From the time the Ottoman Empire conquered Bosnia, they recognized the Bosnians as a "coherent unit" allowing Bosnians to govern themselves within the larger empire.[70] During this time Bosnia formed the Ottoman Empires Western front with the Austro-Hungarian Empire.[71] The Ottoman Empire continued to expand its power into Western Europe, which resulted in Ottoman defeat in the Austro-Ottoman War (1683 to 1699). The war was settled by the treaty of Karlowitz, in which the European powers unified under a common banner, established the Habsburgs as the dominate force in Europe, and eliminated the threat of invasion from the Turks.[72]

The Treaty of Karlowitz effectively halted the Ottoman's expansion into Europe and was a leading cause of the decline of the Ottoman Empire. For the next 175 years the Ottoman Empire was in decline while European power grew. The combination of the decay of their influence and neglect of the people of Bosnia began to have effects on their control of the region. In 1875 the people revolted against the Ottoman nobles in the Peasants Rebellion. The peasants (mainly Christians) revolted against the abuses of the

---

[69]Ibid., 55.

[70]Donia and Fine, *Bosnia Hercegovina*, 72.

[71]Rhoads Murphey, *Ottoman Warfare 1500-1700* (London: University College London Press, 1999), 7-8.

[72]Philip Adler and Randall Pouwels, *World Civilizations: Volume I to 1700*, 5th ed. (Boston, MA: Thomson Higher Education, 2008), 344.

landlords (who were mainly Muslim).[73] The people of Bosnia allied themselves with Serbia; in turn Serbia declared war on the Ottoman Empire with the desire to annex their weak neighbor Bosnia. Serbia formed an alliance with Montenegro and Russia. This coalition declared war on the Ottoman Empire in 1876 and won in 1878. At the end of the war, Bosnia was annexed into the Austro-Hungarian Empire.

The Austro-Hungarian Empire's control of Bosnia can be broken into three phases. During the first phase they focused on the revival of the religious groups in Bosnia. This was an attempt to quell external influences among the people of Bosnia and attempt to unify them as Bosnian. The second phase focused on developing internal Bosnian political parties and granting autonomy to the Bosnian Serbs and Muslims. During this phase the empire officially annexed Bosnia and Herzegovina, but still allowed for the people to develop their own constitution and political parties. The third phase repressed the Bosnian Serbs influence on Bosnia. It was feared that the Bosnian Serbs sought to undermine Austrian efforts in order to join Serbia.[74] The Austrians never truly gained the support of the Bosnian people as a general group, due to their inability to grasp the complexity of the ethnic groups in Bosnia.

The tension between Serbia and the Austrian empire grew in the early twentieth century. A series of diplomatic disputes were won by Austria, but this only furthered the resentment of Serbia and the Bosnian Serbs. Serbia continued to attempt to destabilize Bosnia by sending Serbian nationalists into Bosnia to ferment dissent and unrest. These insurgents planned to attack Archduke Franz Ferdinand, who was heir to the Austrian

---

[73]Donia and Fine, *Bosnia Hercegovina*, 91.

[74]Ibid., 93-115.

thrown, during his visit to Sarajevo in 1914. The assassins came from a Bosnian underground group called Mlada Bosna (Young Bosnia). This group had ties to the Serbian secret society called the Black Hand.[75] The successful assassination and its links to Serbia cause the Austro-Hungarians to deliver an ultimatum to Serbia. The ultimatum was for Serbia to quell all anti-Austrian movements in Serbia and allow Austria to conduct an investigation in Serbia in regards to the murder. Serbia replied that they would attempt to suppress anti-Austrian groups and conduct an internal investigation, but that Austria would not be allowed to enter Serbia to conduct investigations. The response enraged Emperor Franz Josef who promptly declared war on Serbia.[76]

Austria's declaration of war on Serbia caused a chain reaction in which all of the major European powers declared war on each other and divided in two alliances. The two groups were the Central (Germany and the Austro-Hungarian Empire) and Entente (England, France, and Russia) powers. These powers went to war and during WWI millions lost their lives and massive destruction occurred across Europe. This war caused the demise of the Austrian Empire and its control over Bosnia.[77]

At the end of the WWI Serbia, who had sided with the Russians and the other Entente powers, had the upper hand in post-war restructuring. Serbia dominated the political scene and maneuvered its forces into Bosnia and annexed it as part of Serbia in 1918. Croatia and Slovenia, seeking to distance themselves from the Austrian Empire, joined in negotiations with Serbia to form a great Slavic state. On December 1, 1918 the

[75]Ibid., 115.

[76]Ibid., 116-117.

[77]Ibid., 116-119.

"Kingdom of Serbs, Croats, and Slovenes" was created. This new kingdom was designed to be a royal parliamentary system. From the beginning there was conflict in this new parliamentary system between the dominant Serbs and the independent minded Croats. Tensions came to a head in 1928 when five Croats were shot during an argument in parliament. As a result, the king suspended parliament, declared a royal dictatorship, and changed the name of the country to the "Kingdom of Yugoslavia."[78]

The king unified the country and set about to control the political infighting among the political parties and ethnic groups. In 1931, the king reestablished the parliament, but maintained ultimate authority over the kingdom. The king dismantled Bosnia and reformed it into sections that could be controlled by Serbian royal appointments. The Croats were infuriated by the actions of the king and a Croatian fascist group assassinated him during a visit to France in hopes of creating an independent Croatian state. After the death of the king, Prince Paul assumed power of the Kingdom of Yugoslavia. Paul attempted to quell Croatian hostilities by developing a power sharing agreement. At the same time, the kingdom was enhancing its relationship with the fascist regime in Germany. The relationship was largely in the economic sector in which Germany desired to develop heavy manufacturing and mining interests in Yugoslavia. As Nazi Germany and Mussolini's Italy began their expansion, they formed an alliance and invaded surrounding countries. In 1941, Hitler gave the Yugoslavian Government an ultimatum to join in an alliance, which the government agreed. This alliance with the Nazis was not supported by the people, which lead to a coupe by the military. Upon receiving the news about the coupe, Hitler deployed his forces into the kingdom and

---

[78]Ibid., 121-128.

conquered the country in a few days. The opposition forces hid in the countryside and the royals fled to England were they formed a government in exile.[79]

Yugoslavia was now under the control of the Axis powers. In defense of their country two resistance movements were created with different goals. The royalist of the "Yugoslavian Army in Homeland" sought to re-instate the kingdom of Yugoslavia. The rival group, the People's Liberation Front that was dominated by the Communist Party of Yugoslavia headed by Josip Broz Tito sought to establish a communist state.[80] Tito was born to a Croat father and Slovene mother in the village of Kumrovec in then Austria-Hungry. He was an Austrian during WWI, captured and imprisoned by the Russians at a work camp in the Ural Mountains. During his time in Russia he was involved in socialist movements and participated in the Bolshevik Revolution. Once back in Yugoslavia he joined the Communist Party of Yugoslavia. He rose to the top of the party and leveraged his previous military expertise in the defense of his homeland against the Nazis.[81]

During the occupation by the Axis forces Tito mounted a significant resistance movement and with the assistance of Soviet forces was eventually able to force the German forces to retreat from Yugoslavia.[82] After defeating the Axis powers in Yugoslavia, Tito was able to consolidate his power and was installed as the nation's

---

[79]Ibid., 129-135.

[80]Ibid., 137-144.

[81]John Fine, *Balkan Strongmen: Dictators and Authorian Rulers of Southeast Europe* (London: C. Hurst & Co. 2007), 269.

[82]Donia and Fine, *Bosnia Hercegovina*, 154-156.

leader in 1945.[83] Between the years of 1943 to 1946 the country changed its official name from Democratic Federal Yugoslavia, to Federal People's Republic of Yugoslavia , and finally settled on the Socialist Federal Republic of Yugoslavia. The Socialist Federal Republic of Yugoslavia contained six socialist republics: Bosnia and Herzegovina, Croatia, Macedonia, Montenegro, Serbia, and Slovenia.[84]

In the wake of WWII Yugoslavia was in ruins. Its' economy and infrastructure had been decimated by years of occupation and war. Tito turned to the Soviets for help and received limited aide in establishing soviet systems. These systems would have developed Yugoslavia into a satellite state, made dependent on the Soviet Union.[85] Tito continued to struggle with Moscow and Stalin about Yugoslavia's future in the post-war world. As tension rose between the two countries, Yugoslavia was ousted from the Communist Information Bureau in 1948.[86] The Communist Information Bureau was responsible for the creation of the Eastern Bloc system of post-war Europe that made all the satellite countries revolve around the Union of Soviet Socialist Republics (USSR) as the base of power. Now that Yugoslavia was essentially on its own, Tito established Titoism. Titoism was a communist like doctrine that was based on socialism, but independent from external influence by any of the world's major power blocs.[87] Shortly after establishing independence from Moscow, Tito appealed to the US for aide to rebuild

---

[83]Ibid., 158.

[84]Ibid., 161.

[85]Ibid., 165-167.

[86]Ibid., 158.

[87]Ibid., 170.

his country. The US awarded Yugoslavia one billion dollars of various types of aide in 1951. Tito's ability to play both sides of the Cold War allowed him to create the Non-Alignment Movement (NAM). The NAM was formed by unifying countries that refused to side with either the US, NATO, or the USSR's Warsaw Pact.[88] NAM took a stand against colonialism and foreign military installations in sovereign countries.[89] Tito's global influence and ability to have a relationship with both the Eastern and Western power blocs allowed him to maintain control of Yugoslavia until his death in 1980.

In the 1960s and 1970s there was domestic tension in Yugoslavia and the beginning of nationalism. Tito and his regime swiftly dealt with the uprising and removed all nationalist participants from positions of power to ensure that the central power wouldn't be challenged. During his reign in Yugoslavia Tito focused on Titoism, which emphasized developing benefits for his nation and its people as a whole, while opposing external political influences.[90] When Tito died his international influence was illustrated by his funeral. Four kings, 31 presidents, six princes, 22 prime ministers, and 47 ministers of foreign affairs, came from one 128 different countries on both sides of the Cold War to attend his funeral.[91] Tito's ability to shield his country from external political influence and create the illusion of external enemies, gave him the ability to manage internal ethnic conflicts between the people of Yugoslavia.

---

[88]Micah Halpern, *Thugs: How History's Most Notorious Despots Transformed the World through Terror, Tyranny, and Mass Murder* (Nashville, TN: Thomas Nelson, 2007), 253.

[89]Donia and Fine, *Bosnia Hercegovina*, 172-173.

[90]Ibid., 170.

[91]Jasper Ridley, *Tito: A Biography* (London: Constable & Co., 1994), 19.

Yugoslavia after Tito

Tito failed to groom a successor. This was because of his desire not to have any political competitors during his reign. Tito though a dictator, was not as ruthless as Joseph Stalin who purged thousands of his own people. Near the end of Tito's life he developed a new constitution that outlined the process for selecting the Presidium, which would govern Yugoslavia after his passing. The Presidium was a body of 10 people: "the President, Secretary of the Presidium, plus the six presidents of the republican central committees and the two presidents of the provincial committees."[92] This group would select the candidates to be the next president and secretary. Getting all of the competing personalities of the different republics to agree was a task that Tito could manage, but was impossible after his passing. Tito also created term limits and restrictions for the president and secretary once they were elected. The president and secretary couldn't be from the same republic or autonomous region, in order to reduce the chance of one republic gaining an advantage over the others. Once elected, their terms would be limited, the president would serve for a one-year period and the secretary would serve for a two-year period.[93]

The post-Tito system failed to keep Yugoslavia together in the 1980s. Economic problems and the rise of nationalism created cracks in the state that was previously held together by Tito's personality. The weakening of the state and ending of the Cold War set the stage for the death of Yugoslavia.

---

[92]Slobodan Stankovic, *The End of the Tito Era, Yugoslavia's Dilemmas* (Stanford, CA: Hoover Institution Press, 1981), 118-119.

[93]Ibid, 119.

The Destruction of Yugoslavia

Yugoslavia was a country formed by several nations that unified in order to repel external powers. Tito held these nations together with his strategy of unity and brotherhood under a form of communism. Tito was able to maintain unity among the republic for 35 years, but with his death the differences among the republic began to become more and more apparent. The destruction of Yugoslavia was caused up by political, economic, and military factors. The political system that had been successful for so many years relied on a strong central figure to regulate it. Throughout history the ethnic groups of these republics attempted to gain independence and self-determination. In the 1980s several of the republics began to assert themselves, which in turn undermined the strength of the Yugoslavia federal system.

The first series of events that began to erode the political system was revival of Serbian nationalism. This movement was sparked by the release of a 74 page memorandum from the Serbian Academy of Science in 1986.[94] This document claimed that since 1945 and the formation of the post-WWII state of Yugoslavia; the Serbs had been divided and underdeveloped in order to maintain the federal state. The memorandum discussed the establishment of Kosovo as an autonomous province from Serbia 1981, which rekindled the medieval tensions dating from the Battle of Kosovo 600 years earlier. When Kosovo became autonomous the Serbs that lived there feared for their safety and many fled to Serbia. This exodus of Serbs would develop into a call to

---

[94]Carole Rogel, *The Breakup of Yugoslavia and the War in Bosnia* (Westport CT: Greenwood Press, 1998), 18.

arms in order to regain their ancient land in Kosovo that their ancestors had died for hundreds of years ago.[95]

Slobodan Milosevic, who led the Serbian Communist Party in 1987, headed the new Serbian nationalism movement.[96] He stoked the flames of ethnic tensions and used the tension to power Serbian nationalism. When there was a riot in Kosovo by Serbs in 1987, Milosevic created a media spectacle where he was heralded as the protector of the Serbian people. Milosevic's power continue to gain strength until 1989 when he gave a speech to one million Serbs on the site of the Battle of Kosovo for its 600th anniversary. In the speech, he rallied the Serbian people and scared the rest of Yugoslavia with the threat of rising Serbian power.[97]

Slovenia and Croatia saw the writing on the wall and began moving toward independence. In 1990, Slovenia attempted to present reforms to the Yugoslavian Congress, but was confronted by Serbian opposition. Seeing the futility of their efforts the Slovenian delegation left the congress. They were followed by the Croatian delegation. This was the last time that the Yugoslavian Communist Congress ever met.[98] Slovenia and Croatia immediately began to plan for multi-party elections in their own republics. Each country announced their independence from Yugoslavia in 1991.[99]

---

[95]Ibid., 19.

[96]Halpern, *Thugs*, 253.

[97]Rogel, *The Breakup of Yugoslavia and the War in Bosnia*, 20.

[98]Ibid.

[99]Ibid., 20-25.

The second main factor for the destruction of the Yugoslavian state was economics. Yugoslavia was a communist system based on a state run economy that was easily manipulated by Tito. This gave a false sense of economic security, which was bolstered by foreign aide. Since Tito and Yugoslavia had broken away from the USSR's influence, the west had showered them with foreign aide. Yugoslavia never aligned with the West politically, but received aide in order to ensure that they would never re-join the Warsaw Pact. The theory was that if Yugoslavia would not join the West, then at least the West would deny the Soviets access to them. With the end of the Cold War foreign aide to Yugoslavia began to dry up and their international debts became overwhelming. This mound of debt caused hyperinflation, adding to the tension among the nations of Yugoslavia.[100]

The last factor was the military of Yugoslavia and each republic. The majority of the officers in the federal Yugoslavian Army were Serbs. However, each one of the republics had developed a territorial defense force, which was similar to the US National Guard. Both Slovenia and Croatia had the foresight to reinforce their forces against the possibility that Serbia would used military force to keep them from becoming independent.[101]

Wars of Independence

The day after Slovenia declared independence June 26, 1991; the central government deployed its forces to take control of Slovenia. The Slovenian National

---

[100]Ibid., 17.

[101]Ibid., 25-26.

Guard was prepared for a confrontation and defeated the Yugoslavian forces in 10 days with minimal causalities. A truce was brokered in the European Community, Yugoslavia acknowledged Slovenian independence and withdrew its forces. The conflict was so easily concluded because there were so few Serbs in Slovenia and they had always been the most distant member of Yugoslavia.[102] This would not be the case with Croatian independence.

In July of 1991, Yugoslavian forces began to fight the Croatian forces to prevent Croatian independence. Furthermore, the Yugoslavian forces began to support Serb interests in Croatia by defending portions of Croatia that had large Serbian populations. This effectively split the country in half and caused significant civilian casualties. The fighting continued until November 1991 when a UN envoy was able to create a ceasefire agreement. The agreement was signed in the beginning of 1992 and a UNPROFOR was deployed as a buffer between the two armies.[103] The peace in Croatia would hold until 1995 when the Croats launched Operation Storm with the assistance of US and NATO airpower, allowing them to reclaim their land and force the Serbian forces out of Croatia.

<u>The Bosnian War 1992 to 1995</u>

Bosnian attempts for independence were the most violent. Between April 1992 and ending with the signing of the peace agreements on December 14, 1995, Bosnia would see 145,000 (some estimates are as high as 250,000) people killed, 174,000

---

[102]Ibid., 25.

[103]Ibid.

wounded and two and a half million displaced.[104] The reason for the high level of violence was the ethnic makeup of Bosnia, the tactics employed by all sides, Serbian forces posture, and the lack of preparedness by the government of Bosnia for war.

Bosnia had the largest population of Serbs of any of the countries that desired independence and to break ties with Serbian dominated Yugoslavia. Pre-war Bosnia had been the most diverse population of any republic in Yugoslavia with 31.4 percent Serbs, 43.7 percent Muslims, 17.3 percent Croatian, and 5.5 percent claiming Yugoslavs.[105] The Serbian and Croatian populations formed political parties that had agendas that were aligned with their parent countries of Serbia and Croatia. When the vote for independence came to the Bosnian Congress, both the Croats and Muslim population (66.7 percent of the overall voters registered) overwhelming voted (99.7) in agreement. The Bosnia-Serbian political party voted to secede from Bosnia and form the Republic of Srpska. The ethnic lines were now firmly established for the beginning of a multi-sided Civil War within Bosnia.

All sides of the Bosnian War employed tactics against the civilian population. The viewpoint of America, NATO, and the UN when entering the Bosnian conflict, was dominantly one of Serbian aggression and ethnic cleansing against the weak and defenseless Bosnian Muslim population. This viewpoint is very short sighted when the facts are presented clearly. Serbian, Croatian, and Muslim forces conducted ethnic cleansing and what was defined as war crimes against humanity. Each ethnic group

---

[104]Ibid., 73.

[105]Susan Woodard, *Balkans Tragedy* (Washington, DC: Brookings Institute, 1995), 33.

forced out the opposing ethnic groups from places where they held the majority and created detention or ethnic concentration camps.[106]

The Yugoslavia Federal Army was observing a ceasefire with Croatia, being enforced by UNPROFOR in 1992.[107] This gave the federal army time to refit and reorganize their forces. As mentioned before, the majority of the federal forces were Serbian and even though the Yugoslavian Military was forced to withdraw from the area, out of the 100,000 troops, 80,000 remained in the Republic of Srpska because they were Bosnian-Serbs.[108] This clearly gave the Republic of Srpska a military advantage over the Bosnian parent state. Unlike Slovenia and Croatia, Bosnia had not been preparing for war by fortifying its defense and was caught completely off guard. Additionally, the Bosnian leadership was under the impression that the people of Bosnia had co-existed for so long that they wouldn't fall victim to external ethnic tensions. They had not anticipated the problems of the Republic of Srpska.

United States Strategy Toward Yugoslavia

The United States of America had supported the liberation forces of Yugoslavia during WWII. The royal monarch was in exile, his forces were in tatters, and the partisans were conducting an insurgency against the fascist puppet state imposed by Nazi Germany and Muslin's Italy. Similar to the US position with the Soviet Union during WWII, anyone who opposed the Axis powers was an ally and the American war

---

[106]Steven L. Burg and Paul S. Shoup, *The War in Bosnia-Herzegovina: Ethnic Conflict and International Intervention* (Armonk, NY: M. E. Sharp, 1998), 178-181.

[107]Rogel, *The Breakup of Yugoslavia and the War in Bosnia*, 26.

[108]Ibid., 32.

economy pumped as many resources as possible into them, in order to comprise the Axis'

capabilities. Upon the successful expulsion of the Axis powers, Josip Tito was exalted as

the national hero and elected to be the leader of Yugoslavia.

After WWII the world began to be split between the Communist and Capitalist

nations of the world. The USSR headed the Communist nations via the Warsaw Pact and

the United States of America headed the Capitalist nations via the creation of NATO.

From 1945 to 1948 Tito and Yugoslavia fell in the Soviet sphere, but in 1948 Tito created

a rift in his relationship with the USSR's Stalin. Tito wanted to focus on the sovereignty

of Yugoslavia, as opposed to becoming a periphery state to the metrople of Soviet

Moscow. This rift was seen as an opportunity by the West to deny the Soviets influence

in Europe. The US and other western nations awarded Yugoslavia foreign aide and

championed it as a success model for other Soviet states to follow. As mentioned

previously in this chapter this aide in no way aligned Yugoslavia with the western

nations, but was employed to deter Tito from rejoining the Warsaw Pact. To illustrate

Tito's relationship with the world power he co-founded the Non-Alignment Movement.

The principle behind the NAM was to strength third world countries in order to reduce

their vulnerabilities to NATO and the Warsaw Pact.

The US and the western nations continued to try and support Yugoslavia until the

end of the Cold War. The viewpoint of the US can be seen in the National Security

Decision 133 of 1984 by the Reagan Administration.[109] In National Security Decision

133 President Reagan outlined the importance of Yugoslavia as the "southern flank" of

---

[109]White House, National Security Decision 133, *United States Policy Toward Yugoslavia*, President Ronald Reagan. SII 90457, 1984.

the "Soviet expansionism and the hegemony in southern Europe." He mentioned the importance of supporting the Yugoslavia diplomatically, economically, and militarily via military equipment sales. President Reagan also mentioned the important role that Yugoslavia played in regulating NAM and counteracting Soviet and Cuban influence in that organization.

In 1989, with the end of the Cold War the US position toward Yugoslavia began to change. US foreign policy headed by Secretary of State James Baker was dominated by the reunification of Germany, the evolution of the new Russia, and events in the Middle East.[110] The relevance of Yugoslavia on the world's stage had significantly diminished. The only advice that the US offered Yugoslavia from 1989 was to stay unified. This was an effort to reduce the possibly of a conflict that would draw resources needed elsewhere in the world. When the conflicts over independence and ethnic tension began, Baker said, "the US didn't have a dog in the fight . . . and that it was a European problem."[111] With the US dodging any responsibility to intervene in the region the violence continued to escalate.

The US continued to avoid the situation that was developing in Yugoslavia even as the violence increased. As each side committed atrocities on the civilian population, the international community became more and more anxious to get involved. In 1993 Madeline Albright urged US action to quell the violence. Unfortunately, she met solid opposition from General Colin Powell, the Chairman of the Joint Chiefs of Staff (CJCS).

---

[110]David Halberstam, *War in a Times of Peace* (New York: Scribner, 2001), 26.

[111]William Clinton, "Dayton Accords and the Future of Diplomacy," C-SPAN Video Library, http://www.c-spanvideo.org/program/Accordsa (accessed March 28, 2013).

His stance was that he wouldn't allow US troops to be deployed until all other options had been exhausted and clear military objectives had been outlined.[112] His advice was based on the failure of US intervention in Vietnam. This failure caused decades of decay in the US military's image and trust from the public. Powell's generation had fought in Vietnam, took the blame for the failures, and reconstructed the military into the world's premier fighting force. The successes in the Gulf War seemed to validate his policy and kept US troops out of the Balkans until 1995.

Even though the US didn't deploy troops to Bosnia, they did support the UN's mandate #725 and participated in NATO's Operation Provide Comfort, Operation Deny Flight, and Operation Sharp Guard. Operation Provide Comfort was started on 1 June 1992 and was to provide airlift operations, including airdrops, force extraction, and delivery of humanitarian supplies in support of the civilians in Bosnia. Operation Deny Flight monitored and enforced the no-fly zone over Bosnia-Herzegovinia. Operation Sharp Guard monitored and enforced shipping embargos that had been placed on Yugoslavia, Croatia, and Bosnia.[113]

On August 28, 1995 an explosion in the Mrkala Market targeted the civilian population in Sarajevo the capital of the Bosnian state. Bosnia-Serb forces of the Republic of Srpska were credited with conducting this attack. As a result, NATO implemented Operation Deliberate Force, which targeted military assets of the Republic of Srpska. The operation was carried out by missile strikes from NATO ships in the

---

[112]Michael Dobbs, *Madeleine Albright: Against All Odds* (New York: Henry Holt and Company, 1999), 359-360.

[113]Larry Wentz, *Lessons from Bosnia* (Washington, DC: DoD Command and Control Research Program, 1998), 16-17, 20.

Adriatic Sea. The effectiveness and destruction caused by this operation is credited with bringing the key players in the conflict to negotiations for the Dayton Accord.[114]

Dayton Accords

On November 1, 1995 the US hosted delegations from Bosnia, Croatia, Serbia, European Union, Russia, and the US, at Wright-Patterson Air Force Base in Dayton, Ohio. The location was picked in order to isolate the parties and force them to come to an agreement. After three weeks of negotiations consensus was agreed upon that would form the General Framework Agreement for Peace (GFAP) in Bosnia and Herzegovina. On December 14, 1995 the peace agreement was signed in Paris and allowed NATO forces to deploy the IFOR to uphold the measures that had been agreed upon.[115]

---

[114]Ibid., 23.

[115]Joyce Kaufman, *NATO and the Former Yugoslavia* (Lanham, MD: Rowman & Littlefield, 2002), 124-125.

CHAPTER 4

CIVIL AFFAIRS OPERATIONS

IN THE BOSNIAN WAR

In the modern information age, events and news have the ability to spread around the world within minutes. The more horrific and violent the story, the faster it spreads. This was especially the case with the Bosnian War and the evolution of the 24 hour news networks. As the images of atrocities against civilians continued to bombard the world's media outlet, the international community was urged into action. After continued prodding, the Clinton Administration took the lead and orchestrated diplomatic efforts in the creation of the Dayton Accords. Then NATO (and the US) deployed to implement the peace (IFOR), but was dragged into having to stabilize the country (SFOR). In order to maintain a lasting peace, Europe was needed to take the reigns and encourage stability in the region EUFOR.

Goals and Objectives of the Dayton Accords

The governing bodies of Bosnia and Herzegovina (BiH), Republic of Srpska, Croatia, Yugoslavia, the European Union representative, Russia, and the US all signed the Dayton Accords (also called the General Framework for Peace, GFAP) on 14 December 1995. In the agreement Bosnia, Croatia, and Yugoslavia agreed to acknowledge and respect each other's sovereignty. The Accords also settled the disputes among the participants and stipulated that Bosnia would get international support to restore stability, rebuild its country, and lead a federation that included the Republic of Srpska. Croatia regained eastern Slavonia. The Accords also ended the embargo against

Yugoslavia (Serbia). The articles required that the participants comply with restrictions on military forces; the agreement of the Organization for Security and Cooperation in Europe guidelines for regional stability; inter-entity boundaries; internationally supervised elections; recognition of the new constitution of Bosnia; commitment to arbitration to resolve disputes; recognition of international standards for human rights; safe passage for refugees and displaced persons; establish a commission to preserve national monuments; establish a commission for Bosnia and Herzegovina public corporations; civilian implementation; and the establishment of an international police task force.[116] The GFAP was signed in Paris and the next day the United Nations Security Council Resolution 1031 was created to allow for the transition of authority from UNPROFOR to NATO's Implementation Force under Chapter VII of the UN Charter for peace enforcement.[117] IFOR's deployment and activities were named Operation Joint Endeavor, the first deployment of NATO forces to conduct out-of-area operations in 45 years.[118]

Planning the Deployment of the Implementation Force

The IFOR overall concept of the operation, approved by President Clinton was to get in, separate the warring factions, build up the Muslim population capability to defend itself, and get out within a year. The concept greatly underestimated the complexity of,

---

[116]Wentz, *Lessons from Bosnia*, 467-473.

[117]Burg and Shoup, *The War in Bosnia-Herzegovina*, 377.

[118]William Buchanan, Robert Holcomb, A. Martin Lidy, Samuel Packer, and Jeffrey Schofield, *Operation Joint Endeavor-Description and Lessons Learned (Planning and Deployment Phases)* (Alexandria, VA: Institute for Defense Analyses, 1996), 1.

and time needed for the task. The Clinton Administration had already seen similar missions fail in Somali and Haiti, where the military redeployed before stability had been achieved.

Even though IFOR had limited time, the GFAP and CH VII gave them the ability to conduct peace enforcement, which was significantly more authority than UNPROFOR's previous mission of peacekeeping. The change in terminology gave the IFOR Commander, US Admiral Leighton W. Smith Jr., the ability to maneuver his forces freely, less restrictive rules of engagement, and the ability to enforce GFAP within the country of Bosnia Herzegovina. The commander of IFOR was also empowered to employ enhanced military capabilities, which in this case was the US 1st Armored Division. To the US this heavy-handed approach was critical, because the military wanted to ensure that it had the capability to overwhelm the former combatants if hostilities arose. During planning for the deployment of IFOR the focus was on deploying a short-term force with significant combat power, instead of planning for a long-term force with stability operations capabilities.

The IFOR looked at the deployment of forces in terms of combating a military problem and created three areas of operations that would be delegated to allied commanders. These were designated as Multi-National Divisions (MND)-North led by the US; the British led MND-South West; and the French led MND-South East.[119] IFOR's planning was centered on achieving the military goals of the Dayton Accords set forth in Annex 1A and identified multiple tasks including: "ensuring self-defense and

---

[119]Robert F. Baumann, George Gawrych, and Walter Kretchik, *Armed Peacekeepers in Bosnia* (Fort Leavenworth, KS: Combat Studies Institute Press, 2004), 120-121.

freedom of movement, supervise selective marking of the Inter Entity Boundary Line

(IEBL) and Zones of Separation (ZOS) between the parties, monitor and enforce the

withdrawal of forces and establishment of the ZOS, control the airspace over Bosnia and

the movement of military traffic over key ground routes, establish Joint Military

Commissions that would serve as the central bodies for all parties to the Peace

Agreement, and assist with the withdrawal of UN forces not transferred to IFOR."[120]

During the planning process IFOR had only one civil affairs planner to assist in the

operations plan. This was indicative of a lack of understanding and emphasis on CAO.

This lack of importance of CA—CIMIC—CMO planning would later been seen as a

detriment to the effectiveness of IFOR during the transition from UNPROFOR.[121]

Implementation Force

On the 16th of December 1995, IFOR deployed it forces as part of Operation

Joint Endeavor from all over Europe to the Bosnian Theater in support of the Security

Council Resolution 1031. IFOR's mission was to implement the military aspects of the

Dayton Accords 1A. IFOR wanted to distinguish itself from a peacekeeping force by

creating the term "implementation force," conveying the message that these forces were

to be actively seeking resolution to the conflict.

The IFOR's organization structure was unique because it was the first time NATO

had to create an organization for "out-of-area" operations. The authorities for this

---

[120]LTC Peter Corpac, "Operation Joint Endeavor: An Artillery Battalion Commander's Experience in Bosnia" (Personal Experience Monograph, U.S. Army War College, 1998).

[121]Wentz, *Lessons from Bosnia*, 129.

operation originated with the North Atlantic Council, which tasked the Supreme Allied Commander Europe. The Supreme Allied Commander Europe and his staff at Supreme Headquarters Allied Powers Europe managed the strategic level operations during the conflict. The Supreme Allied Commander Europe tasked Allied Forces South's Commander Admiral Leighton Smith to be the operational level and IFOR commander. Smith identified Allied Rapid Reaction Corps (ARRC) to be the land component commander IFOR.[122] IFOR's forces totaled around 60,000 troops during the operation.[123] IFOR's troops came from 32 countries. IFOR created three areas of operations MND-North, MND-South West, and MND-South East to be headed by NATO commanders. MND-North, also known as Task Force Eagle, was led by the US and based in Tuzla. MND-North was of the largest international divisions with 22,500 soldiers in 14 brigades (to include 3 international brigades) from 11 different nations.[124] MND-South West was led by the British with troops from Canada, Holland, and Denmark, based in Banja Luka. MND-South East was led by the French with Italian and Portuguese troops supporting them, and based in Mostar.[125] There was much confusion in the logistics during the deployment due to competing efforts and unclear command and control relationships.[126]

The IFOR's main tasks were to separate the warring factions by creating Zones of Separation, create cantonment areas for their arsenals, and then inventory and monitor

---

[122]Ibid., 36.

[123]Burg and Shoup, *The War in Bosnia-Herzegovina*, 377.

[124]Baumann, Gawrych, and Kretchik, *Armed Peacekeepers in Bosnia*, 94.

[125]Wentz, *Lessons from Bosnia*, 36.

[126]Baumann, Gawrych, and Kretchik, *Armed Peacekeepers in Bosnia*, 70-78.

these arsenals to ensure that the violence was ended. Once in Bosnia the IFOR forces began to establish the Zones of Separation between the warring factions. This step could have been very hazardous. It required IFOR forces to displace local military units peacefully. In most cases, all sides complied with the resolution and removed their forces to cantonment sites that were subject to inventory and regular inspections.[127] It was thought that the warring factions complied, because by the time IFOR was deployed they were exhausted from years of inescapable violence. IFOR conducted these operations evenly among the warring parties and quickly established legitimacy in assigned areas with few discrepancies. There was one case where the operations didn't go as smoothly as elsewhere.

Mt. Zep is a mountain in the Republic of Srpska that was a known hideout for the internationally wanted war criminal General Ratko Mladic. During a fly over by allied aircraft, it was noticed that there were unauthorized heavy weapons in the vicinity. Mladic's apprehension was a requirement of the Dayton Accords, but was not a military objective, it was seen as civilian or governance objective. Understanding this, the local IFOR command allowed the local Bosnian-Serb military faction to have autonomy patrolling this 50 square kilometer area, in order to keep the peace.[128] But now that forbidden weapon systems had been identified in the area, action needed to be taken. When IFOR assets went to the area to conduct inspections, the local military refused them access and stated that they would never allow Mladic to be captured.[129] In addition,

---

[127]Ibid., 95-97.

[128]Ibid., 105.

[129]Ibid., 106.

the local Bosnian-Serb population massed at the same location and began to harass the IFORs. The IFOR then coordinated with the president of the Republic of Srpska, Biljana Plavsic in order to utilize her legitimacy to mediate this situation.[130] But the local Bosnian-Serbs that were involved were loyal only to Mladic. This situation continued to develop and became an international news story. Both sides tried to control the story for their own benefit.[131] In the end, through persistence, a show of force, and by adhering to strong self-discipline, the IFOR personnel did gain access. The locals and the Bosnian-Serbs gained a better understanding of IFOR during this standoff. Each side learned to what lengths the other would go before resorting to in violence.

Over the course of the IFOR deployment stability in the region and compliance increased, because the warring factions knew that the opposing forces were also incompliance and the threat of attack was minimal.[132] By June of 1996, IFOR had accounted for the all the heavy weapons and their locations, and was regularly inspecting them.[133] There were a few instances where local military units refused to allow IFOR personnel to conduct inspections. These instances were designed to test the resolve of the IFORs.[134] In all, IFOR conducted itself professionally and competently and was able to enforce the necessary system of the Dayton Accords without using significant force. The

---

[130]Ibid., 112.

[131]Ibid., 111.

[132]Richard L. Holbrooke, *To End War* (New York: Random House, 1998), 278.

[133]Brigadier General Stan Cherrie, "Task Force Eagle," *Military Review* (July 1997): 70-72.

[134]Baumann, Gawrych, and Kretchik, *Armed Peacekeepers in Bosnia*, 104-114.

ability to manage this difficult initial situation gained IFOR legitimacy in the international community and among the factions of BiH and the Republic of Srpska.

During IFOR, Civil Affairs units were limited in their tasks and capabilities. The CA mission during the IFOR was to support the military objectives laid out in the Dayton Accords 1A. At the beginning of IFOR the majority of the major tasks were in terms of offensive and defensive operations. CA assets mainly conducted a liaising role and were in a large part, the staffs at the headquarters for IFOR, ARRC, and Task Force Eagle.[135] This might have been due to the fact that the initial pool from which to draw CA personnel was either Active Duty or Reserve CA personnel, that were already mobilized for something else.

Civil Affairs doesn't deploy in traditional units, instead CA typically deploys in small groups of augmentees from various units. This is evident when looking at the deployment and mobilization orders for IFOR, most orders listed units that were tasked with providing less than 10 personnel for the mission. As mentioned before a large portion, about 100 personnel or 30 percent of all CA and CIMIC resources in country were retained at higher headquarters in staff elements.[136] With this being the first deployment of NATO forces, there were several examples of confusion in the command relationships and responsibilities between the IFOR, ARRC, and MNDs. The main problem was identifying the roles for the IFOR and ARRC staff, and at the same time ensuring that the MNDs were getting the support that they needed from IFOR and being

---

[135] Wentz, *Lessons from Bosnia*, 131.

[136] Ibid.

properly integrated into a larger plan.[137] At the MND level the CA and CIMIC assets were organized according to the country's doctrine. In MND-North, US CA was organized into teams and pushed down to the battalion commanders to be utilized as they chose. In MND-South West the British saw CA and CIMIC as an inherit duty for all military personnel, but developed a coordination cell that was integrating efforts within MND-South West. In MND-South East the French used the military police and other organic assets in support of civilian related fields (logistics, communication, and medical).[138] Thus, across IFOR CMO was organized and conducted differently in each MND.

With IFOR's focus of operations on military objectives, CA didn't play a large role in what would be considered the major events of IFOR's deployment. This is due in part that CA was traditionally considered a function utilized in support of rear-area operations; fear of mission creep; and do to over bearing force protection requirements. The purpose of the traditional CA role in support of rear-area operations was to reduce the chance of disruption in lines of communication and to ensure freedom of movement for friendly forces. The fear of mission creep in regards to targeting civilian objectives is seen time and time again in the Bosnian War. The overbearing force protection measures from higher headquarters required at least a four-vehicle per convoy for all movement, which limited CA units' freedom of movement and their ability to conduct operations. This same limitation effected Psychological Operations (PSYOP) and Information Operations (IO) units. The units attempted to resolve these limitations by reorganizing

---

[137]Ibid., 130-132.

[138]Baumann, Gawrych, and Kretchik, *Armed Peacekeepers in Bosnia*, 192.

CA, PSYOP, and IO units into "company or platoons-sized elements" in order to be able to meet higher headquarters' force protection requirements.[139] This measure was only partly successful.

During IFOR, CA and other units took it upon themselves to develop relationships with non-military entities in order to facilitate the civilian objectives of the Dayton Accords and accomplish various missions. During moments of hostilities, CA personnel coordinated with local leaders, civilians, and the media to ensure transparency of IFOR's intent.[140] Also, they continued to develop the civilian environment to foster the possibilities of peace and the return of normalcy for the local population.

The final task for IFOR was to conduct the national elections. The Dayton Accords required that new national elections be held and the international community saw this as one of the most crucial aspects to measure the effectiveness of IFOR and the GFAP. There were restrictions stating that candidates could not be on the war criminals list, but their parties could still run for office. The results of the election were clearly along ethnic lines and were a form of continued ethnic tensions via non-military means.[141] CA participated in the election and played a critical role through the distribution of information about the election, assisted in coordination with civilian entities, and monitored the election process.[142] Realizing that ethnic discord remained a

---

[139]Ibid., 103.

[140]Baumann, Gawrych, and Kretchik, *Armed Peacekeepers in Bosnia*, 189.

[141]Ibid., 120-123.

[142]Ridge, *Civil Affairs in Bosnia*.

major problem even as the IFOR mission ended; NATO, the US, and the UN decided to extend the peacekeepers mandate with the transition from IFOR to the SFOR.

Stabilization Force

In December of 1996, in the wake of the results of the September elections in Bosnian, the UN authorized the SFOR to be the successor of IFOR. SFOR's mission was to "continue to deter renewed hostilities, stabilize and consolidate the peace and contribute to a secure environment" with the tasks of "preventing the resumption of hostilities; promote a climate conducive to pushing the peace process forward; and providing selective support to civilian organizations within its capabilities."[143] SFOR had the authority to conduct "peace enforcement" under the UN Charter's Chapter VII, giving SFOR's commander's enhanced rules of engagement.

With the transition to SFOR came a restructuring of forces and a reduction in troop strength to 31,000.[144] The bulk of the troop reduction came from each one of the MNDs. There was also a restructuring of the organization of SFOR. One change was the removal of competing and-or redundant Headquarters of IFOR and ARRC. In addition, command relationships were clarified to ensure that the SFOR commander fell directly under the Supreme Headquarters Allied Powers Europe Commander.[145] As the years progressed and the mandate continued to be renewed without any combat deaths or

---

[143]*SFOR Procedural Guide*: Book 1, The Planning Process (Camber Corporation, Killeen, TX: September 1999), 3-2.

[144]Burg and Shoup, *The War in Bosnia-Herzegovina*, 378.

[145]Baumann, Gawrych, and Kretchik, *Armed Peacekeepers in Bosnia*, 123-124.

60

instances of violence, troop numbers continually decreased in 1997, 1999, and 2000. The SFOR transitioned to a new command, EUFOR, in 2004.

The major task for SFOR was the transition of its mission to focus on the civilian objectives of Dayton. At the beginning of the SFOR mission this was a struggle for commanders, who considered it "mission creep" (the expansion of a project or mission beyond its original goals).[146] However, with the insistence of the US Secretary of State Warren Christopher and the US Secretary of Defense William Perry, the SFOR leadership was forced to take action.[147] This led SFOR to include the Office of High Representative's and Organization for Security and Cooperation in Europe once they were fully operational, into the command structure and integrate them into the military's missions. SFOR began to realize that the tool of choice in stabilization or peace operations was not the combat elements of the command but rather the tools of influence and information. This was mainly the Civil Affairs, Information Operations, and Psychological Operations units.

The CA mission under SFOR was to integrate CA and CIMIC efforts into the larger SFOR campaign plan. This was done by SFOR's combined joint CIMIC staff section (CJ9) developing an overall CA campaign plan. The campaign plan that was developed synchronized the efforts of the MNDs into one overarching effort, instead of them working under the guidance of the individual MND commanders. CA efforts were

---

[146]Merriam-Webster.com, "Mission Creep," http://www.merriam-webster.com/ dictionary/mission creep (accessed October 18, 2013).

[147]Holbrooke, *To End War*, 337.

critical to the SFOR mission. Eventually, the Bosnian War would be seen as the time that "Civil Affairs came of age, especially for NATO and the framework of nations."[148]

The CA and CIMIC assets were reorganized in SFOR. The two main improvements were the reduction of staff sections (IFOR and ARRC) as mentioned before and the creation of the Combined Joint Civil Military Task Force headed by US Brigadier General William Altschuler. Altschuler was determined to maximize CA and CIMIC efforts and assets in SFOR and leverage CA toward overall mission accomplishment. He devised three tasks for his new Combined Joint Civil Military Task Force: integrate all CA and CIMIC assets and synchronize all CA efforts, create a civil affairs campaign plan, and develop measures of effectiveness to ensure that SFOR was properly directing its efforts toward mission accomplishment.[149]

The CA's major challenge under SFOR was the changing of CA and CIMIC efforts from a supporting task to the command's main effort. CA did this by gaining the operational initiative, coordinating with non-military entities, and integrating itself with the other tools of influence. With the IFOR to SFOR transition came the focus on stabilizing Bosnia. This was no longer a standard military-to-military problem set. The new campaign was a hybrid of military and civilian objectives. These new objectives came with a host of new participants: military, government, non-governmental, and international organizations which all had important roles. CA played a critical role in bringing all these pieces together.

---

[148]Wentz, *Lessons from Bosnia*, 441.

[149]Baumann, Gawrych, and Kretchik, *Armed Peacekeepers in Bosnia*, 199.

During the transition from UNPROFOR to IFOR, the lack of CA involvement caused an ineffective handover from the UN personnel and the contacts that they had developed during their time in Bosnia. This was a missed opportunity to better integrate the international organizations and NGOs into NATO operations at the beginning of the occupation in Bosnia. Once deployed in theater CA and CIMIC units created local networks and then developed CIMIC centers (US doctrine would call them Civil Military Operations Centers (CMOCs)) at all levels of commands to handle these relationships, which became the critical cogs in stability and peace operations. These centers proved to be very successful in coordinating and conducting meetings to unify the efforts of the Office of High Representative, United Nations High Commission for Refugees, the Organization for Security and Cooperation in Europe, International Committee of the Red Cross, the World Bank, hundreds of International Organizations, NGOs, Private Volunteer Organizations, and various other non-military entities.[150] Many of these organizations lacked solid internal hierarchical structure, which made integration into the international stability initiatives of the Dayton Accords difficult. The individuals at the local level, in a grass roots style, operated these organizations. This allowed them great flexibilities, but this made it difficult for them to be able to coordinate their efforts into a larger operating picture, allowing them to maximize their contributions and increase their ability to reach a large amount of people in need. Additionally, many of these entities had never developed relationships with any military organization. These civilian organizations were unfamiliar or uncomfortable with the process of conducting operations with the military and uncomfortable with the inherently regimented approach

---

[150]Wentz, *Lessons from Bosnia*, 136.

of the military.[151] The CIMIC (or CMOC) centers became a "clearinghouse" for both military and civilian needs in order to foster an environment for stability in Bosnia.[152] They mitigated many of the shortfalls of some of the International Organizations, Private Volunteer Organizations, and NGOs.

During SFOR's development of influence and information operations the IO staffs, PSYOPS, and CA units reinforced and supported others efforts. One of the best examples of this mutually supporting relationship during SFOR was the mine awareness program. IO developed an overarching campaign to alert the civilian population of the dangers of mines. PSYOPS developed a media message to be broadcasted over the local radio and TV stations. PSYOPs also created mine awareness messages to be printed in comic books and on soccer balls. CA supported this effort by distributing these products via their local networks, schools, and directly to children while conducting assessments and civil reconnaissance.[153]

Civil Affair's performance in SFOR was exemplary. The ability of CA units and staffs to overcome obstacles was remarkable. CA personnel and units were highly motivated, more so when allowed to conduct CA operations, CMO, or CIMIC. CA units deployed to Bosnia began to conduct operations by coordinating and executing projects in support of the civilian population. The major problem was that CA was a new

---

[151]Baumann, Gawrych, and Kretchik, *Armed Peacekeepers in Bosnia*, 197.

[152]Thijis W. Brocades Zaalberg, *Soldiers and Civil Power* (Amsterdam, Holland: Amsterdam Press, 2006), 280-282.

[153]Major Steve Larsen, interview with Major Don Phillips and Dr. Robert Baumann, February 18, 1999, in *Armed Peacekeepers in Bosnia*, by Robert F. Baumann, George Gawrych, and Walter Kretchik (Fort Leavenworth, KS, Combat Studies Institute Press, 2004).

capability that commanders didn't fully understand. Most of the professional military training of commanders, focused on effective offensive and defensive operations to meet the enemy on the battlefield, destroy them, and minimize losses. Stability or peace operations were not something that most military leaders were enthusiastic about. Stability was seen as a task that someone else (Department of State or USAID) had to accomplish. Stability operations are characteristically the long-term, complex, dynamic, and not very glamorous in military communities. CA and CIMIC in Bosnia, particularly during IFOR, units were hampered by commander's lack of emphasis on CA-CMO-CIMIC on the battlefield, excessive force protection measures, missed opportunities of integration with IO-NGOs-HN, frustrated and competing command relationships, and conflicting doctrine among allies. Despite these setbacks CA-CMO-CIMIC operations and units were able to achieve considerable successes and to dramatically improve capabilities. This permitted CA to begin to take a leading role in SFOR. Admiral Leighton Smith, Commander of IFOR, recognized the dramatic progress, he stated; "In November (1995), we had never heard of CIMIC, we had no idea what you did . . . now we can't live without you."[154]

European Forces

The CA and CIMIC units continued to play a vital role in SFOR until its transition of authority to the EUFOR in 2004. In SFOR rotations more and more of the responsibilities for stabilization and reconstruction were moved to civilian bodies such as the Stability Pact, United Nations High Commission for Refugees, and the Organization

---

[154]Joint Chiefs of Staff, Joint Publication (JP) 3-57, *Civil Military Operation* (Washington, DC: Government Printing Office, 2013), III-1.

for Security and Cooperation in Europe. These bodies focused on the diplomatic, informational, and economic aspects of the stabilizing and reconstruction effort of BiH. This has allowed EUFOR to carry on with the mission to "maintain a safe and secure environment, and to provide capability-building and training support to the BiH armed forces."[155] As of 2013, EUFOR continues to maintain an operational headquarters element in BiH and relies on "over-the-horizon" deployment of troops in a time of need. In 2013, EUFOR exercised those relationships in "Exercise Quick Response 1 and 2." During the exercise the EUFOR tested its capabilities to absorb and operate operational forces; to conduct casualty evacuation; exercise crowd control measures; transport and support a multinational force with "over-the-horizon" capabilities; deploy two light infantry companies (Austria and Slovakia); and enhanced and validated the Armed Forces of Bosnia and Herzegovina, and military capabilities in a multinational task force.[156]

The events that happened in Bosnia might have been avoidable or at least the human suffering could have been reduced. It is assumed that if NATO and the US had acted sooner a significant amount of bloodshed could have been avoided. It is impossible to change our history, the only course of action we have is to learn from history and ensure that we apply its lesson to the current and future events.

---

[155]EUFOR, "EU Military Operation in Bosnia and Herzegovina (Operation EUFOR ALTHEA)," http://www.euforbih.org/index.php?option=com_content& view=article&id=15&Itemid=134 (accessed October 18, 2013).

[156]Ibid.

CHAPTER 5

MEASURE OF EFFECTIVENESS OF US CIVIL AFFAIRS AND CONCLUSION

The employment of US Civil Affairs capabilities in Bosnia was a success despite the need to overcome multiple complications. It is difficult to develop metrics that can quantify the successes of CA in the Bosnian War. Additionally, it would be misleading to point to the measures of progress (measure of performance, which is a quantitative measurement) that are direct results of CA efforts as the sole reason for a lasting stability in Bosnia. This is a common problem with CA on the battlefield. One could point to the amount of work conducted by CA in post war Germany and Japan, and conclude that they only reason these countries are currently (2013) economic power houses and regional leaders is due to the post war CA efforts. In both of these cases there were so many contributing factors to their current status it would be very misleading to assume that CA is the sole reason for the successes. What can be said with out a doubt is that CA has played a critical role in the US ability in increasing stability during the post-war efforts in Germany and Japan. This can also be said for Bosnia. CA developed relationships and liaised between non-military entities that were the staples of the stability effort in post-war Bosnia. CA was a major factor contributing to the political, military, economic, and social well being that has maintained the peace for over a decade in Bosnia. This chapter will dive deeper into the information used to support these findings by analyzing the key components of the Bosnian War. These components are the Dayton Accords, IFOR, SFOR, and the effects that the Bosnian War had on civil affairs.

The Dayton Accords

First and foremost in the analysis of the Bosnian War, it is necessary to understand the creation and execution of the Dayton Accords. The Dayton Accords succeeded in stopping the violent deconstruction of the former state of Yugoslavia and the civil wars that erupted as a result. Unfortunately, it was only a short-term fix to a long-term problem.

During the Bosnian War and the eventual destruction of the former Yugoslavia, the ethnicities of Bosnian and Herzegovina were influenced by external powers. The external powers created the ethnically centric countries of the Republic of Srpska (backed by Serbia) and the Croatian Republic of Herzeg-Bosnia (backed by Croatia) within the boarders of BiH. The heads of these external powers were signatories of the Dayton Accords. One of whom, Serbian leader Slobodan Milosevic, later stood trial for war crimes against humanity. The other signatory, President of Croatia Franjo Tudjman is widely to be believed to have had a hand in orchestrating the Croats actions when they conducted ethnic cleansing. These new countries soon dominated parts of BiH and conducted atrocities that forced migration of ethnic populations, in order to form ethnically pure regions. The intent was that these regions would be absorbed into the neighboring countries at a later date. All sides (Serb, Croat, and Bosnian) of the war conducted these terror style tactics, unlike the popular belief that only the Serbs resorted to such extremes. By giving legitimacy to these newly formed countries within the internationally recognized borders of BiH and allowing their sponsors to participate in the Dayton Accords, the international community facilitated the continuation of ethnic tension within a once peaceful nation. During the mediations at Dayton, these

68

discrepancies should have been addressed and the notion of supporting the reunification of these countries under one single governing body, Bosnia, should have been a priority.

In the end, the Dayton Accords effectively established an end to the violence. But, in doing so it created a divided country to be governed by multiple entities that continually sacrificed progress for their own political interests.[157] As opposed to making a confused and frustrating situation clear, the Dayton Accords actually created additional layers of bureaucracy and unnecessary levels of government, which slowed the process of development and reconciliation within Bosnia. The Dayton Accord effectively created conditions on the ground that inhibited the success of the military mission. These had to be overcome by the military commanders with the assistance of the CA leaders.

Implementation Force

At the strategic level, the deployment of IFOR was a success. It was supported by the international community, under a UN resolution in support of military action under Chapter VII, to conduct peace enforcement in order to end the violent atrocities being carried out on civilians, and was designed to meet a strictly ethical and altruistic end. IFOR was able to form a coalition of willing nations across alliances such as NATO, non-NATO, and even countries opposed to NATO. It was then able to deploy a large multinational force from various locations and organize them into multinational commands.

---

[157]Kemal Kurspahic, "From Bosnia to Kosovo and Beyond: Mistakes and Lessons," in *War and the Change in the Balkans: Nationalism, Conflict and Cooperation*, ed. Brad K. Blitz (New York: Cambridge University Press, 2006), 85.

Once in BiH, IFOR conducted peace enforcement operations, ended the violence, quickly separated the warring faction with zones of separation, and established a weapons monitoring program. The warring militaries obeyed the terms of the peace agreement and complied with IFORs peace enforcement operations. IFOR then supported the BiH elections to establish a legitimate government, under the new constitution mandated by the Dayton Accords. This government was to conduct a transition of authority from IFOR, in order to complete the goals of the Dayton Accords. The results of the first election illustrate that ethnic tensions were still very strong and a continuing military presence was required.

The IFOR was successful at completing its military objectives. However, a lack of strong leadership in Washington resulted in deployment of military assets with the possibility of getting involved in missions outside their "mission essential tasks;" with a lack of accountability and participation from the US diplomatic community; and a lack of understanding of the requirements to make BiH a stable nation. Ignoring these factors contributed to a lengthy commitment to BiH that should have been realized by the American national and military leadership at the national security level.

This situation had happened before with the initial outbreak of hostilities in the former Yugoslavia. Madeline Albright and other influential civilian entities had pressed the White House to act militarily in the defense of the people of Bosnia. The President consulted his senior military advisor, General Colin Powell (CJCS), who insisted that all diplomatic channels had to be exhausted before a military option could be explored. Powell, recalling his experiences in the Vietnam War, advised that the military should only be used for a short duration, with overwhelming force, and to attain clearly stated

70

military objectives. There would also need to be a diplomatic mission that would be responsible for reconstruction efforts led by the Department of State and supported by other (non-Department of Defense) governmental agencies. This sobering military viewpoint in developing national strategies is the task of the CJCS. Additionally, the CJCS is required to advise the President on his military options, assist the President to understand the capabilities of his forces, assist the President to establish clear goals for the military, and to ensure that other governmental agencies understand their role in any possible military actions. Powell's advice reflected the limited view of US military commanders of CA and CA capabilities. It also was indicative of the US military's post-Vietnam cultural aversion to "nation building."

In 1995, when the violence against civilians and non-compliance of the UN mandates occurred in BiH, there was significant push back from the military community regarding the option to deploy US troops. The military sited the same reasons that Powell had previously stated. Unlike before there was a different CJCS, General Shalikashvili. He had a different viewpoint of the situation. In 1995 the CJCS sided with the non-military government agencies and the White House decided to deployed forces. Still, the CJCS and the President were under the misconception that the military would accomplish their narrow military objectives and redeploy within a year.

This misunderstanding of being able to redeploy within a year and not be concerned about conducting stability operations trickled down throughout the planning process of IFOR. It reinforced the US military's cultural view of nation building. One of the most apparent examples of this was that IFOR had only one civil affairs planner to assist in the operations plan.[158] The subsequent history provides perspective on the

magnitude of this error. Over the course of operations in Bosnia US forces conducted less

than 120 days of offensive and defense operations and almost nine years conducting

stability operations, but initially only had one planner to even attempt to consider stability

operations. In today's doctrine there are whole staff sections dedicated to phases of

stability and transition to civil authority. This lack of importance of CA-CIMIC-CMO

planning not only reduced the military tasks for CA forces, but also negatively effected

the deployment of CA units, manning, and logistical requirements.

The early lack of understanding of CA and CA capabilities had cascading effects,

due to the fact that at that point in time (1995) 96 percent of all US civil affairs forces

were reservists that would need to be mobilized, which takes months. The CA personnel

had to be mobilized to be available for planning before operations began. Without

significant CA planning ability, IFOR's plan failed to include the NGOs that were

already in country.[159] UNPROFOR had already established a working relationship with a

significant amount of the NGOs that had been already working in Bosnia. If CA planners

had been properly integrated in the planning process they could have deployed a

coordination element to conduct a proper handover. This would have ensured that the

NGOs capabilities were integrating into the overall IFOR campaign plan. These

additional capabilities would have enhanced the chance of success in overall stability

efforts, even if the military would not be specially responsible for its execution. Finally,

lack of CA-CIMIC-CMO involvement in the planning reduced the utilization and

---

[158]Wentz, *Lessons from Bosnia*, 129.

[159]Ibid., 135.

implementation of civilian agencies, governmental and non-governmental, from around the world that could prepare for follow-on post-IFOR efforts of stability and the transition of BiH to be a functioning state once again.

Stabilization Force

During SFOR CA began to "come of age" and was quickly recognized as the most critical asset of stability operations. CA went from strictly a "rear-area" capability to the main effort for stability operations. For eight years CA units rotated through BiH with most CA soldiers conducting multiple rotations. This experience was priceless for CA personnel, doctrine, creditability, and illustrated the level of importance of CA to the US military community. These efforts slowly began to change US military cultural as well as doctrine. These changes resulted in updated US Civil Affairs doctrine and an awareness of the importance of CA among US senior military leaders.

Under SFOR, CA and CIMIC units worked tireless to create civil projects and programs that fostered an environment that would increase the overall stability of BiH. Many of the projects that were developed assisted in the transition to EUFOR in 2004. EUFOR has been instrumental in maintaining the peace and is now the main focus of the efforts in Bosnia, fostering economic and political development. These efforts in development can be seen in the formation and inclusion into the Stability Pact for South Eastern Europe, which transitioned to the Regional Cooperation Council in 2008. The Regional Cooperation Council's priority is to bring BiH to the level of a viable candidate for European Union membership. Membership in the European Union could result in a level of political and economic stability that BiH has never known. Enhanced CA capabilities in SFOR were the key to a successful hand-over of the stability mission from

SFOR to EUFOR. Additionally, they were the key capability to continue BiH's political stability under both SFOR and EUFOR.

Affects of the Bosnian War on the Civil Affairs Community

To answer the question "was CA effective in the Bosnian War," it is important to take an operational snapshot of then and now in order to conduct an analysis of the difference. This analysis enables the identification of the effects that the Bosnian War had on CA. The best way to analyze the difference is to utilize the Army's DOTMLPF framework. DOTMLPF stands for: Doctrine, Organization, Training, Material, Leadership Development, Personnel, and Facilities.

The Bosnian War affected Doctrine both for US Civil Affairs and NATO Civil Military Cooperation. The Bosnian War justifying the need to maintain the capabilities that were already stated in CA doctrine. For NATO CIMIC it justified the need to develop this capability to reduce confusion among their member countries. For CA operations during the Bosnian War the US doctrine was more that adequate. When reviewing FM 41-10 it is difficult to see any major discrepancies that need to be addressed. One area that has been developed as a direct result of the Bosnian War can be found in the most recent FM 3-57, *Civil Affairs Operations*, dated 2011. FM 3-57 discusses the importance of integration of CA with IO for overall mission success. The doctrine also states that CA efforts need to be nested with PSYOP efforts into an overarching IO campaign. Additionally current doctrine requires that these efforts should be incorporated with other governmental agencies, international organizations, and NGOs through a Civil Military Operations Working Group. The Civil Military Operations

Working Group concept was successfully utilized during recently operations in Iraq, Afghanistan, and the Philippines, to create a "whole-of-government" approach.[160]

The countries that participated in IFOR and SFOR also had doctrinal issues when it came to CIMIC-CMO-CAO or peace and stability operations. The United Kingdom looked at these types of operations as an inherit part of all other operations; this is due in part to the decades of operations in Northern Ireland.[161] This experience allowed the United Kingdom to rely on all of its soldiers and leaders to conduct CIMIC-CMO-CAO during their directed mission without specialized assets. The French viewed CIMIC-CMO-CAO as two parts; one is liaising and the other is direct support to civilian projects. The French view towards CA and CIMIC was very similar to that of the US.[162] During the organization of US Civil Affairs forces in IFOR and SFOR, in the French controlled MND-South East they politely declined US Civil Affairs personnel and opted instead to utilize their own organic assets.[163] Most of the other partner nations viewed these operations as the role of a mediator and observer. On the other end of the spectrum of peace operations, the Russian's would only support tasks that were clearly outlined in the Dayton Accords. This outlook made the Russian focus their efforts on peace enforcement to the point of conducting counter-insurgency operations.[164]

---

[160]U.S. Department of the Army, FM 3-57, 4-15–4-16.

[161]Matthew Midlane, *Britain, NATO, and the Lessons of the Balkans Conflict 1991-1999* (London: Frank Cass, 2005), 181-200.

[162]Wentz, *Lessons from Bosnia*, 127-128.

[163]Ibid., 127-130.

[164]Ibid., 125-127.

The North Atlantic Treaty Organization was developed to defend Europe against possible aggression from foreign militaries. With the collapse of the Soviet Union, NATO's role has been redefined. In the time between the end of the Cold War (1990) and the deployment to Bosnia, that role was uncertain. The nations of NATO focused on combat operations as part of the Cold War. During the Cold War NATO developed plans to conduct a type of stability operation, in case of a catastrophic collapse of the Soviet Union, the Eastern European countries, and Eastern Germany. With the end of the Soviet Empire, these capabilities were deemed to be no longer necessary. Some countries in NATO had participated in peace operations under the UN banner, but each country still created their own doctrine. In addition, when deploying to Bosnia, most participants expected a deployment that would last a year and then expected to terminate military involvement. The view of IFOR was similar to the US view.

Bosnia was NATOs first CIMIC centric mission in its history; it is understandable that the doctrine wasn't properly integrated. Since the deployment of forces to Bosnia, NATO has created an approved doctrine that is taught at the NATO Civil-Military Co-Operation Centre of Excellence. US Civil Affairs forces are familiarized with this doctrine at the John F. Kennedy Special Warfare Center and School. This gives both NATO and US Civil Affairs knowledge of each other's terminology and doctrine. However, there still is a need to streamline efforts and develop common doctrine, thus reducing confusion or frustration in an operational environment. The current US Civil Affairs leadership has been attempting to reduce friction with allies by constructing real world scenarios that will enhance US capabilities with partner nations. This was recently seen in the 85th Civil Affairs Brigade's participation with Australian CIMIC units during the exercise Talisman Sabre 2013 and corresponding personnel exchanges between the two units.

The Bosnian War affected the CA "Organization" aspect of DOTMLPF by justifying the need to enlarge the size of Active Duty CA units. During the Bosnian War there was one Active Duty CA BN. This was the 96th CA BN. Each of the battalion's companies were regionally aligned, and a major part of its leadership were special forces (SF) soldiers that usually were only in the CA field for a few years and then returned to the SF community. The departure of these personnel back to the SF community continued to deplete the knowledge, expertise, and experience from the Active Duty CA. Since the Bosnian War the CA community has expanded significantly. The first expansion was the addition of the 95th Civil Affairs Brigade (Airborne) and then most recently the addition of the 85th CA Brigade.

The 95th CA Brigade consists of five regionally aligned special operations CA BNs. The 91st CA BN (A) is regionally aligned to United States Africa Command and Special Operations Command Africa. The 92nd CA BN (A) is regionally aligned to United States European Command and Special Operations Command Europe. The 96th CA BN (A) is regionally aligned to United States Central Command and Special Operations Command Central. The 97th CA BN (A) is regionally aligned to Asia and typically deploys in support of United States Pacific Command and Special Operations Command Pacific. The 98th CA BN (A) is regionally aligned with South and Central America and typically deploys in support of United States Southern Command and Special Operations Command South.

The structure of a 95th CA Brigade (A) has a command group, five battalions, CMOC, civil affairs planning team, and headquarters company. The commander of a CA Brigade is a Colonel assisted by a commander Sergeant Major (typically from the special forces branch). The CMOC can be found at every level of CA command from a CA Company to the CA Brigade. It is responsible for coordinating, planning, supporting, and monitoring all CAO for its supported unit. At the Brigade level the CMOC has a Civil Liaison Team, which is used as a "national-level to international level"[165] element to interact with senior military and civilian leaders. The CMOC at the Brigade and BN levels has a CIM Team that is responsible for collecting all the data that the units generate, ensure that it is properly maintained, and incorporated for future missions. The civil affairs planning team is utilized at the theater level as a "plug and play" planning asset. The civil affairs planning team can be quickly deployed, fill the immediate requirements, and create a plan for additional forces to be deployed for an enduring solution. The headquarters company is responsible for support garrison operations. All of these capabilities are the results of lessons learned from Bosnia.

The 85th Civil Affairs Brigade (85th CA BDE), is stationed at Ft. Hood Texas, falls under FORSCOM, and supports general purpose forces missions. The 85th CA BDE is structured in the same fashion as the 95th CA BDE, and has regionally aligned battalions. The main difference is that the 85th CA BDE lacks airborne assets. Currently (2013) the military is going through a restructuring process and it is unknown if the 85th CA BDE will survive in the future. Creation of the 85th BDE reflects the understanding

---

[165]Ibid.

that CA is not just a mission associated with SF operations. This is also a lesson of Bosnia.

During the Bosnian War, 96 percent of the force structure of CA units and personnel were in the reserves. The Active Duty CA unit was only a functional area and didn't become an official branch until 2006. CA currently has two active duty brigades with regionally aligned battalions. These brigades have the capability to rapidly deploy elements that could have coordinated with the UNPROFOR, NGOs, and the civilian population. These elements would have developed the civil military operating picture for IFOR. They would have also acquired information that would have driven the mobilization cycle and pre-mission training models for the reserve and follow on, civil affairs units. This would have ensured that the right capabilities were deployed to the right place, at the right time. The increase in the active component of CA addresses the planning and mobilization issues identified in the IFOR deployment.

The Bosnian War affected the CA "Training" aspects, by validating the need to have both CA generalist and specialist. Active Duty CA personnel are typical generalist and usually focus on identifying the underlining cause of the problem set, then cultivate the resources that are required to solving the problem. Reserve CA retains CA specialists that are experts in their various civilian fields. These specialists were a large reason that CA gained so much positive notoriety during the Bosnian War. These specialists were able to apply their skill set immediately to the effected population with little or no additional technical assistance.

The Bosnian War affected the Civil Affairs Material component in two important areas. The first was the need to acquire systems that are able to analyze the civil environment for their commanders and the second was the ability to modify force protection requirements. Improvements in both of these areas have been critical to modern CA operations and can be directly linked back to CA operations conducted during the Bosnian War.

Most analytical capabilities are organic to a unit and are focused on immediate or emerging kinetic threats, placing the civil layer of the battlefield at a very low priority. After CA's successes in the Bosnian War, it was identified that CA needed to be able to conduct analysis of their operations to support the larger mission. This justification has led to a myriad of systems and products, each focused on developing the civil aspects of the common operating picture. These capabilities continue to be very challenging to master, because the information that CA gain, analyze, and the products that they produce, would be best suited to be shared with civilian agencies and non-governmental entities. Producing useful analytics is still problematic. This is partly due to operations security and classification requirements which restrict information distribution to allies and civilian agencies.

Force Protection requirement are designed to protection the soldier from acknowledged threats in the operation environment while conducting operations. In IFOR and then SFOR, US commanders focused on maintaining an unnecessarily high level of force protection that was dictated by higher headquarters. All US forces were required to wear Kevlar (helmets) and flak jackets when on missions and all movements were required to use four-vehicle convoys with crew served weapons (heavy machine guns) when leaving their bases. This aggressive posture was designed to make US personnel "hard" targets and deter any hostilities from possible combatants. These convoy requirements made it difficult for CA assets to conduct operations, due to their small size. At the lower levels the CA units tried to make due by combining with other specialized units that were in a similar situation (IO and PSYOP). In 1997, the convoy requirements were reduced to a two-vehicle convoy, but the individual equipment requirement remained. This unnecessary measure of protection hindered CA effectiveness. By seeming to always be ready for a serious fight, CA units had a difficult time putting the civilians they interacted with at ease. European partners, in contrast, were authorized to determine their force protection requirements at the lowest level of leadership. This allowed them to interact with the local populace with a more open and friendly approach, which led to a better ability to gauge the local climate.[166]

The Bosnian War affected the Leadership Development within CA and the military by bringing to light the lack of understanding that the military leadership had of civil affairs and how to employ them. The most obvious example was when Admiral Leighton Smith (Commander of IFOR) said, "In November (1995), we had never heard of CIMIC, we had no idea what you did . . . now we can't live without you."[167] This was a United States Admiral, who "had no idea," what CA was or how to effectively employ CA units. The case can be made that he was in the Navy and his career was focused on naval operations. As an Admiral who has been given the command of a joint and combined force, IFOR, he should have had knowledge of the joint forces and their

---

[166]General Sir Rupert Smith, Kermit Roosevelt Lecture (24 September 2001, US Army Command and General Staff College, Fort Leavenworth, KS); Student and faculty comments to George Gawrych, September 2001, in *Armed Peacekeepers in Bosnia*, by Robert F. Baumann, George Gawrych, and Walter Kretchik (Fort Leavenworth, KS: Combat Studies Institute Press, 2004).

[167]Joint Chiefs of Staff, JP 3-57, III-1.

capabilities under his command. The case can also be made that after Bosnia senior leaders should understand the importance of CA and its application on the battlefield. The important lesson of CA integration, demonstrated in BiH, was not finally learned until the US was in the midst of Operation Iraqi Freedom 10 years after IFOR deployed. The application of CA and stability operations should be introduced at all levels of military professional development. In today's age of the strategic corporal it is important for each soldier to understand how their actions (positive and negative) will affect overall operations. Additionally, company grade officers should receive training on the aspects of CA and stability operations. Company grade field artillery officers should get enhanced training, due to the fact that they are typically tasked to be the battalion S9 (Civil Affairs staff officer) in stability operations. Finally, CA and stability operations should be a focal point for commanders during their Pre-Command Course, Pre-Mission Training, and have a case study that focuses on CA and stability operations at the Command and General Staff College and War College. It is too late to train a commander and his staff on how to integrate CA into stability operations when they arrive in country.

The Bosnian War affected the CA "Personnel" component with the creation of the 38-series MOS. This MOS falls under Special Operations Command and is maintained by the United State Army Special Operations. This has been one of the most critical developments for the CA community. One benefit of falling under the control of Special Operations Command and United States Army Special Operations is that the conventional Army doesn't manage active duty CA personnel. This benefits the CA Branch and personnel by allowing them to avoid being reduced by the lack of priority that CA might have in generating a conventional force that is focused strictly on fighting

82

and winning America's next conventional battle. Typically in developing the forces the focus is on Combat Arms capabilities and an accepted marginalization of specialized capabilities that are not kinetically forced.

The Bosnian War affected the CA "Facilities" by keeping them close to other United States Army Special Operations units. The bulk of CA unit's maintain garrison facilities at Fort Bragg, North Carolina, and also rely heavily on the resources that are there for their specialized training. An example of this specialized training is the language and culture training that CA personnel receive at the United States Army John F. Kennedy Special Warfare Center. This training is done in conjunction with PSYOPS and SF personnel. This reduces the overall cost to the military and has allowed for the development of personal relationships between the individuals of these different branches during their training. Additionally being centered at Fort Bragg, CA takes advantage of integrating training opportunities with PSYOP, SF, and the 82nd Airborne Division. These training activities are usually simulations of quick reaction, real world, current threat based situations. By having all these units being collocated at the same facility this reduces the cost of having to transport units, increases training opportunities for each of these communities, and facilitates an environment that encourages cross-pollination of skills sets that will be required for future engagements.

Conclusions

Civil Affairs was effective in Bosnia. Before the Bosnian War CA was seen as a task of rear-area operations. In the Bosnian War, CA and stability operations emerged as tasks that were as critical as offensive and defensive operations. This was evident during the transition from IFOR to SFOR and the emphasis on stability operations. In IFOR the military came in and achieved its military objective swiftly, but there was much more that needed to be done. The additional objectives relied on CA-CIMIC-CMO capabilities to accomplish them.

This importance of CA, post-Bosnian was illustrated by the increased focus on CAO and CMO in operations around the world. The Operation Enduring Freedom-Philippines' mission is currently focused on conducting 80 percent of the operations under the CAO and CMO title. CAO and CMO's development and use of non-lethal tactics to influence the indigenous population and marginalize threat groups is a direct result of the success in Bosnia. Also the increased amount of CA forces in the US military's inventory was a direct result of the Bosnian experience. With the operational understanding of the need to ensure stability in nations and regions post conflict, CA has become a critical asset. The US military has realized that after the war is won there is a need to conduct another step in order to achieve "mission accomplishment." This next step is stability operation, which requires a well-trained CA force. CA is absolutely critical to transitioning from military occupation to the host nations civil administration. This isn't a process that happens quickly or falls within standard military operations, doctrine, and procedures. It is a process that requires many factors and CA has shown that it has the ability to manage them to achieve mission success.

Civil Affairs needs to continue to properly market itself to the military community. Currently CA units are conducting operations all over the world. The bulk of active duty CA personnel are based at Fort Bragg, North Carolina, which has become the center for the CA community. Within the last few years the 85th Civil Affairs Brigade was created at Fort Hood, Texas. The 85th CA BDE, will create battalions that will be based on several large Army installations in support of the regionally aligned general purpose forces.[168] Additionally, there are many CA staff positions in commands around the world. Unfortunately, with Fort Bragg as the center of the universe for CA, most of the positions outside Fort Bragg are looked down upon and some consider them to be bad for their career. This attitude reduces the amount of quality personnel that are interested in supporting the rest of the general purpose forces, especially at staff positions. These staff positions are critical to ensure that commanders are well versed in the CA-CAO-CMO skills, capabilities, and how to employ them. The quote from Admiral Smith mentioned before is as much the fault of the CA community, as his own. As a community, CA needs to ensure they are sending our best individuals to fill key staff positions to ensure operations are being conducted with CA-CAO-CIMIC-CMO incorporated in them. By integrating well trained and quality officers early into the planning process, commands will reduce the possibility of the situation that happened with IFOR, which had only one CA planner and no overarching plan for CA.

In Thomas Barnett's, *The Pentagon's New Map*, he discusses the creation of a stability force that focuses on the transitional period between war and peace. He refers to this organization as the "System Administration Force (SAF)."[169] This force would be able to transition from the conventional military conducting war; and have the capabilities designed to conduct stability and the transition to the HN or civilian framework. Most of the civil affairs core tasks would be able to be incorporated in to this

---

[168]U.S. Department of the Army, FM 3-57, 2-2.

[169]Thomas Barnett, "Let's Rethink America's Military Strategy," *TED talks* Filmed February 2005, http://www.ted.com/talks/thomas_barnett_draws_a_new_ map_for_peace.html (accessed October 21, 2013).

System Administration Force framework. CA is already at the forefront of conducting operations with the interagency community. CA has developed a successful track record working with USAID, Department of State, Department of Agriculture, and other agencies.[170] Additionally, training with partner nation's militaries and civilian agencies will increase their overall capabilities and reduce US troop requirements. This line of effort should be as important in the national strategy as shipping lane security, counter-terrorism, and Weapons of Mass Destruction related issues. If the leadership has the foresight to see the demand for stability operations, we will need to properly train with our regional allies in the diplomatic, information, military, and economic arenas. Developing this capability will allow the US and our allies to resolve issues of stability quickly and expend significantly less capital, in both men and money.

America is a great nation and has the most powerful military mankind has ever seen. However, it can't, even if it tried, fix all the world's problems. This is why it is important for CA to develop interdependent relationships with other governmental agencies, international organizations, and regional partners. This needs to be incorporated into training, prior to operational missions being identified. By creating partnerships through CA the US military can develop new ways to handle international issues without large-scale assistance from the US. Allowing regional partners to play a critical role in assisting each other increases regional stability and interdependency, as opposed to the US attempting to solve all the world's problems. The US military develops these relationships by professional education exchange programs, combined exercises, and liaison officers. CA takes it a step further by developing their personnel into regional

---

[170]U.S. Department of the Army, FM 3-57, 1-6–1-7.

experts with training in language, culture, and various other non-military fields. By fostering these relationships the US military builds capabilities and develops personal relationships that have the ability to supersede policy or national interests.

As the world develops, it actually becomes smaller. In the past, it was relatively easy for countries to ignore happenings on the other side of the world and revert to isolationism. With the dawn of the information age and the need to constantly increase economic growth, this idea of being able to shut off the rest of the world has become as much a thing of the past as the horse and buggy. CA units are the military's ultimate tool for interacting with the civil world outside the US

> There will be other Bosnias in our lives–where early outside involvement can be decisive, and American leadership will be required. The world's richest nation, one that presumes to great moral authority, cannot simply make worthy appeals to conscience and call on others o carry the burden. The world will look to Washington for more than rhetoric the next time we face a challenge to pose.

> — Richard Holbrooke, *End of War* 369.

BIBLIOGRAPHY

Adler, Philip, and Randall Pouwels. *World Civilizations: Volume I to1700*. 5th ed. Boston, MA: Thomson Higher Education, 2008.

Andrade, Dale, and James H. Willbanks. "CORDS/Phoenix: Counterinsurgency Lessons from Vietnam for the Future." *Military Review* (March-April 2006): 9-23.

Barnett, Thomas. "Let's Rethink America's Military Strategy." *TED talks.* Filmed February 2005. http://www.ted.com/talks/thomas_barnett_draws_a_ new_map_for_peace.html (accessed October 21, 2013).

Baron, W. "Civil Affairs United States of America." *CIMIC Messenger* 5, no. 1 (March 2013). http://www.cimic-coe.org/download/newsletter/CIMIC-Messenger-2013-01-final.pdf (accessed July 13, 2013).

Baumann, Robert F., George Gawrych, and Walter Kretchik. *Armed Peacekeepers in Bosnia.* Fort Leavenworth, KS: Combat Studies Institute Press, 2004.

Buchanan, William, Robert Holcomb, A. Martin Lidy, Samuel Packer, and Jeffrey Schofield. *Operation Joint Endeavor-Description and Lessons Learned (Planning and Deployment Phases)*. Alexandria, VA: Institute for Defense Analyses, 1996.

Burg, Steven L., and Paul S. Shoup. *The War in Bosnia-Herzegovina: Ethnic Conflict and International Intervention*. Armonk, NY: M. E. Sharp, 1998.

Carson, Colonel Jayne A. "Nation-Building, The American Way." Strategy Research Project, United States Army War College, Carlisle Barracks, PA, 2003. http://www.fas.org/man/eprint/carson.pdf (accessed October 19, 2013).

Cherrie, Brigadier General Stan. "Task Force Eagle." *Military Review* (July 1997): 70-72.

Clinton, William. "Dayton Accords and the Future of Diplomacy." C-SPAN Video Library. http://www.c-spanvideo.org/program/Accordsa (accessed March 28, 2013).

Corpac, LTC Peter. "Operation Joint Endeavor: An Artillery Battalion Commander's Experience in Bosnia." Personal Experience Monograph, U.S. Army War College, 1998.

DiMarco, Louis A. "Restoring Order: The US Army Experience with Occupation Operations, 1865-1952." Ph.D. Diss., Kansas State University, 2010.

Dobbs, Michael. *Madeleine Albright: Against All Odds*. New York: Henry Holt and Company, 1999.

Donia, Robert J., and John V. A. Fine. *Bosnia Hercegovina: A Tradition Betrayed*. New York: Columbia University Press, 1994.

EUFOR. "EU Military Operation in Bosnia and Herzegovina (Operation EUFOR ALTHEA)." http://www.euforbih.org/index.php?option=com_content& view=article&id=15&Itemid=134 (accessed October 18, 2013).

Fine, John. *Balkan Strongmen: Dictators and Authorian Rulers of Southeast Europe*. London: C. Hurst & Co., 2007.

Halberstam, David. *War in a Times of Peace*. New York: Scribner, 2001.

Halpern, Micah D. *Thugs: How History's Most Notorious Despots Transformed the World through Terror, Tyranny, and Mass Murder*. Nashville, TN: Thomas Nelson, 2007.

Hicks, Kathleen, and Christine Wormuth. *The Future of U.S. Civil Affairs*. Washington, DC: Center for Strategic and International Studies, 2009. http://csis.org/files/ publication/130409_Hicks_FutureCivilAffairs_Web.pdf (accessed July 14, 2013).

Holbrooke, Richard L. *To End War*. New York: Random House, 1998.

Joint Chiefs of Staff. Joint Publication (JP) 3-57, *Civil Military Operation*. Washington, DC: Government Printing Office, 2013.

Kaufman, Joyce. *NATO and the Former Yugoslavia*. Lanham, MD: Rowman & Littlefield, 2002.

Kurspahic, Kemal. "From Bosnia to Kosovo and Beyond: Mistakes and Lessons." In *War and the Change in the Balkans: Nationalism, Conflict and Cooperation*, edited by Brad K. Blitz, 76-86. New York: Cambridge University Press, 2006.

Malcolm, Noel. *Bosnia A Short History*. New York: New York University Press, 1994.

Merriam-Webster.com. "Mission Creep." http://www.merriam-webster.com/ dictionary/mission creep (accessed October 18, 2013).

Midlane, Matthew. *Britain, NATO, and the Lessons of the Balkans Conflict 1991-1999*. London: Frank Cass, 2005.

Murphey, Rhoads. *Ottoman Warfare 1500-1700*. London: University College London Press, 1999.

Oehrig, Cristen. *Civil Affairs in World War II*. Washington, DC: Center for Strategic and International Studies. http://csisdev.forumone.com/files/media/csis/pubs/ 090130_world_war_ii_study.pdf (accessed July 13, 2013).

Ridge, Eric. *Civil Affairs in Bosnia*. Washington, DC: Center for Strategic and Internal Studies. http://csis.org/files/media/csis/pubs/090129_bosnia_case_study.pdf (accessed November 5, 2013).

Ridley, Jasper. *Tito: A Biography*. London: Constable & Co., 1994.

Rogel, Carole. *The Breakup of Yugoslavia and the War in Bosnia*. Westport, CT: Greenwood Press, 1998.

SFOR Procedural Guide: *Book 1, The Planning Process*. Killeen, TX: Camber Corporation, September 1999.

Shatziller, Maya. *Islam and Bosnia: Conflict Resolution and Foreign Policy in Multi-Ethnic States*. Ontario, Canada: McGill-Queen's University Press, 2002.

Smith, General Sir Rupert. Kermit Roosevelt Lecture, September 24, 2001, US Army Command and General Staff College, Fort Leavenworth, KS.

Special Operations History Foundation. "Objective Security." Recorded 1945. United States Marine Corps. film strip. http://specialoperationshistory.info/omeka/items/show/124 (accessed May 21, 2013).

Stankovic, Slobodan. *The End of the Tito Era: Yugoslavia's Dilemmas*. Stanford, CA: Hoover Institution Press, 1981.

U.S. Department of the Army. Field Manual (FM) 3-05.40, *Civil Affairs Operations*. Washington, DC: Government Printing Office, October 2006.

———. Field Manual (FM) 3-57, *Civil Affairs Operations*. Washington, DC: Government Printing Office, 2011.

———. Field Manual (FM) 41-10, *Civil Affairs Operations*. Washington, DC: Government Printing Office, 1993.

Ushistory.org. "The Fall of the Roman Empire." http://www.ushistory.org/civ/6f.asp (accessed August 22, 2013).

Villinger, Audrey. *Civil Affairs in the Korean War*. Washington, DC: Center for Strategic and International Studies. http://csis.org/files/media/csis/pubs/090130_korea_study.pdf (accessed July 14, 2013).

Wentz, Larry. *Lessons from Bosnia*. Washington, DC: DoD Command and Control Research Program, 1998.

White, Jeremy Patrick. *Civil Affairs in Haiti*. Washington, DC: Center for Strategic and International Studies. http://csis.org/files/media/csis/pubs/090130_haiti_study.pdf (accessed November 5, 2013).

White House. National Security Decision 133, *United States Policy Toward Yugoslavia*. President Ronald Reagan. SII 90457. 1984.

Woodard, Susan. *Balkans Tragedy*. Washington, DC: Brookings Institute, 1995.

Zaalberg, Thijis W. Brocades. *Soldiers and Civil Power*. Amsterdam, Holland: Amsterdam Press, 2006.

www.ingramcontent.com/pod-product-compliance
Lightning Source LLC
Chambersburg PA
CBHW080316290526
45790CB00005B/2063